CLINGING

The Experience of Prayer

Emilie Griffin

eighth day
BOOKS
Wichita, Kansas

Eighth Day Press, 2838 East Douglas, Wichita, Kansas 67214

Cover design by NetWerx Creative, Inc.

The author wishes to thank the following for permission to use quotations: for 80 verses from *The Jerusalem Bible*, copyright © 1966 Darton, Longmans, Todd and Doubleday & Company, Inc. Reprinted by permission of the publisher. For eight lines from *Selected Poems and Letters of Emily Dickinson*, copyright © 1959 by Robert N. Linscott; reprinted by permission of Elizabeth Linscott.

THIRD EDITION

Library of Congress Cataloging-in-Publication Data:

Griffin, Emilie
CLINGING: THE EXPERIENCE OF PRAYER
Originally published: San Francisco: Harper & Row, © 1984.
Second edition: New York, New York: McCracken Press, a trademark of Multimedia Communicators, Inc. © 1994.
ISBN 0-9717483-3-0
LCCN 2003104354
1. Prayer–Christianity 2. Experience (Religion) 3. Title

For

DORIS
MICHAEL
TERRY
JOHN

with hoops of steel

Contents

My God, what is a heart,
that thou shouldst it so eye, and woo,
Pouring upon it all thy art,
As if that thou hadst nothing else to do?
Teach me thy love to know,
that this new light, which now I see,
May both the work and workman show;
Then by a sunbeam I will climb to thee.

—GEORGE HERBERT

Foreword

There is no explanation for another book on prayer except perhaps the one found at the end of John's Gospel, saying that if one were to include everything Jesus ever did, the world could not contain the books that would be written.

Prayer, I suspect, is part of what Jesus Christ has done in me, and for that I most gratefully make this effort to share that treasure.

As for "clinging," I have consciously chosen an image of attachment to God, in hopes of conveying our dependency on him. I mean it, too, as a metaphor of detachment: the true clinging that sets us free from the many false dependencies that bind us hand and foot.

William Johnston writes in *Silent Music* of clinging both true and false:

It would be relatively easy to abandon our clinging fixations if they were in the conscious mind. But more often they are not. . . . Often such relationships are partly projections: we are imposing our father and mother images upon others, clinging to others as a child clings to its parents. . . .[1]

Purification from all such clinging is necessary, yet when we arrive at nonattachment, we have not yet arrived. A further movement of faith is necessary:

So [the meditator's] great stability continues to stem from the knowledge that he is loved . . . not faith that I am loved *because* I am good and holy and sinless; it is my belief that I am deeply loved in spite of my sinfulness. . . . Yahweh does not love his people because they are holy but in order to make them holy. And this is the faith the meditator clings to in his journey through the profound caverns of the unconscious. . . .[2]

In another place Johnston says the mystic must cling to God ("for God is his truest being"), but need not cling to views and ideas about God.[3]

I hasten to say that by clinging I intend to convey the experience of prayer, not any special sort of method or discipline.

Instead, what I have written is an experiment. I have set out to draw a picture of prayer from the perspective of one person. The hope is that its very singularity will strike a more general chord.

Within the metaphor of clinging I want to describe several aspects of prayer. But these ought not to be thought of as stages or steps. Instead, they are facets of the one jewel, some random gleams issuing from that precious stone.

If they were cards, it would be possible to deal them out in any order and still have the description make sense. Even the first chapter, "Beginning," might as easily be read last, for as Newman rightly said, "We are ever but beginning."

While I do not intend to write a spiritual how-to book, I have nevertheless used as a model that sort of how-to book one finds in art stores, which shows how to draw flowers or cats. Such books are filled with sketches of simple things. In the same way, I am trying to sketch prayer from a number of vantage points.

Clinging is not an account of my prayer life, but a picture drawn *from* life of an experience that is both elusive and vivid, exotic and familiar. I think I am something like Audubon, wanting to capture in the wild something that will not thrive in captivity.

The metaphor holds true in another sense, too. To glimpse this experience, one must learn to keep still.

I said that "clinging" was both my own and borrowed. Recently I found it in a small essay by Karl Rahner on prayer:

Love is a complete pouring out of oneself, a total clinging from the last depths of one's being.[4]

He describes the experience even better when he says:

You have seized me; I have not "grasped" you. You have transformed my very being right down to its last roots and made me a sharer in your own Being and Life.[5]

Thomas Aquinas writes of clinging when he treats happiness and the will:

The will of one who sees God's essence must cling to God (*Deo inhaeret*) for then out of necessity we must will to be happy. . . .[6]

And Augustine uses the same word precisely in the *Confessions*:

When at last I cling to you with all my being, for me there will be no more sorrow, no more toil. Then at last I shall be alive with true life, for my life will be wholly filled by you.[7]

NOTES

1. William Johnston, *Silent Music: The Science of Meditation* (San Francisco: Harper & Row, 1979), p. 142.
2. Ibid., p. 119.
3. William Johnston, *The Still Point: Reflections on Zen and Christian Mysticism* (New York: Fordham University Press, 1970), pp. 179–80.
4. Karl Rahner, *Encounters with Silence*, trans. James M. Demske (Paramus, N.J.: Newman Press, 1960), p. 22.
5. Ibid., p. 30.
6. St. Thomas Aquinas, *Summa Theologica*, Ia, q.82, a.2,3 (Madrid: Biblioteca de Autores Cristianos, 1961), p. 577.
7. St. Augustine, *Confessions*, Book X, 28, trans. R. S. Pine-Coffin (Harmondsworth, Middlesex, England: Penguin Books, 1961), p. 232.

1. Beginning

There is a moment between intending to pray and actually praying that is as dark and silent as any moment in our lives. It is the split second between thinking about prayer and really praying. For some of us, this split second may last for decades. It seems, then, that the greatest obstacle to prayer is the simple matter of beginning, the simple exertion of the will, the starting, the acting, the doing. How easy it is, and yet—between us and the possibility of prayer there seems to be a great gulf fixed: an abyss of our own making that separates us from God.

To make matters worse, we can approach the abyss that lies between us and prayer and retreat from it under cover of being-too-busy or having-family-obligations or even serving-God-in-other-ways. This seemingly justified retreat makes the approach more difficult the next time until there is at last, before beginning, a beginning of beginning, and so on *ad infinitum*. A mud wall is built by the crawfish claws of our reluctance, hardened into clay, baked by the passage of time, till at last it seems too difficult to break down.

What is even more insidious is that we think we are praying all the time we are not. We are in God's hands at all times, we tell ourselves. We acknowledge his greatness. All our actions are shaped and formed by him. We assure ourselves that we are of course very open to prayer while not actually praying. We congratulate ourselves that we are so well-intentioned about prayer that we don't actually have to pray! This whole line of reasoning is like nothing so much as the alcoholic's assurance to himself that he only drinks for pleasure, on rare occasions, or the smoker's insistence that he can take tobacco or leave it alone. Yet, in some part of ourselves, we know our delusions.

I do not mean to judge another person's heart. I am speaking only for all the unprayerful persons I have been. The fears I describe are my own fears at one time or another in my experience of prayer.

Why should we feel this reluctance, this hesitation—when we sense, or know, or guess, that prayer is one of the most exquisite possibilities on earth?

Don't we know what the poets have to tell us about prayer? George Herbert writes:

> Prayer, the Church's banquet, Angels' age,
>   God's breath in man returning to his birth,
>   The soul in paraphrase, heart in pilgrimage
>   The Christian plummet sounding heaven and earth;
> Engine against the Almighty, sinners' tower,
>   Reversed thunder, Christ-side-piercing spear,
>   The six-days world transposing in an hour,
>   A kind of tune, which all things hear and fear;
> Softness, and peace, and joy, and love, and bliss,
>   Exalted manna, gladness of the best,
>   Heaven in ordinary, man well dressed,
>   The Milky Way, the bird of paradise,
> Church-bells beyond the stars heard, the soul's blood,
>   The land of spices; something understood.[1]

Four centuries later, his words still ring true and clear, inviting us to pray. Yet this deep attraction is accompanied by hesitation. And that is very natural.

Prayer is, after all, a very dangerous business. For all the benefits it offers of growing closer to God, it carries with it one great element of risk: the possibility of change. In prayer we open ourselves to the chance that God will do something with us that we had not intended. We yield to possibilities of intense perception, of seeing through human masks and the density of "things" to the very center of reality. This possibility excites us, but at the same time there is a fluttering in the stomach that goes with any dangerous adventure. We foresee a confrontation with the unknown, being hurt, being frightened, being chased down.

Don't we know for a fact that people who begin by "just praying"—with no particular aim in mind—wind up trudging off to missionary lands, entering monasteries, taking part in demonstrations, dedicating themselves to the poor and sick? To avoid this, sometimes we excuse ourselves from prayer by doing good works on a carefully controlled schedule. We volunteer for school committees, to be readers in church or youth counselors, doing good works in hopes that this will distract the Lord from asking us anything more difficult. By doing something specific and limited "for God," something we judge to be enough and more than enough, we skirt the possibility that God—in prayer— may ask us what he wants to ask, may suggest what we should do.

"Father, into your hands I entrust my spirit." Isn't that one of the most disturbing sentences in the Scriptures? We know God asks hard things. We know he did not spare his own Son. We know Jesus prayed, not now and then, but all the time. Isn't this what holds us back—the knowledge of God's omnipotence, his unguessability, his power, his right to ask an All of us, a perfect gift of self, a perfect act of full surrender?

Prayer, we tell ourselves, therefore, is not for us. Or, if it is for us, it is surely not the same thing for us as it is for those specially called to religious life. Doesn't God understand that we have other bonds—marriage, parenthood, concern for our own parents—holy bonds that release us from the necessity for all this prayer?

Deep down, however, we know that God is asking us to pray. Why else would we feel this constant prompting, this sense of disenchantment with things, this knowledge that there is always something just beyond the hill, something that will fill the empty places in us and make our lives complete?

"I don't want your holocausts. I don't want your burnt offerings. All I want is you." Deep within we know that God is not asking a heroic time-commitment, but a giving of the heart. He is taking away, one by one, all the excuses and defenses we can invent. He does not demand long prayer periods, visible penances, giving things up. (A few are sometimes called to these, and when they are, they run to make the gift.) What God mostly asks is that we pray in secret and sincerely. How we go about it is up to us.

I once had a friend who was inclined to be overweight but always wanted to be thin. One day she confessed to me her motivation. The thought in her mind always was, "I'll fix *them*. I'll get fat." Fatness was her response to personal hurts and rejections. It is sometimes the same in our relationship to God.

"I'll fix him. I won't pray." But who is really the loser by this rejection of God's love? In prayer, what the Lord offers us is an intense perception of his tenderness and care. We may insist that when we pray we don't feel anything at all. But we should also be honest enough to admit that when we don't feel anything, it may be because of the walls we have built to protect ourselves against rejection, the layers, the walls, the defenses against the possibility of being hurt. To remove these barriers in prayer takes time and will not come in a moment or a day.

We may have built walls against prayer, against the presence of God, because of things he has not given us, things we thought we deserved. We may be blind to the blessings he has given us and think only of those he has withheld. We may be refusing to enter into any mentality that accepts loss and defeat as trials given for our growth and perfection. We may be refusing to pray because we don't intend for God to have it his way.

Yet in spite of all this, in some part of ourselves, we know our delusions, our denials. Prayer, we sense, is a way of coming back to what is true and real. There is courage in it. And we want the courage to face the boundedness of our existence and move beyond it, to cast off the crippling effects of fear and anger, to break through barriers of space and time. Can prayer really accomplish these things? If we are Christians, we know it can.

Prayer is a move out of bondage into freedom, the bold move of those who are willing to die now instead of waiting till the time comes. It is casting off shackles, deliverance, passing through prison walls. In prayer, Shakespeare's reality is turned inside out. Prayerful Christians die many times before their deaths, trusting never to taste of death at all. Christians in prayer die into something: the possibilities of God's love. They take the gamble that Christ has overcome death and that life is not impossible with God.

And prayer is the perfect remedy for world-weariness. We who are accustomed to complex problems and suspicious of simple remedies doubt prayer because it is so obvious. It stares us in the face. It is like the clue overlooked by Scotland Yard because it has been sitting on the coffee table all the while. Only the master sleuth is open-minded enough to consider that such an obvious clue is the real one.

To pray means to be willing to be naive. People who pray are really the laughing-stock. Anyone knows (anyone being someone who knows hardly anything about it) that prayer is the refuge of the old and the rejected, the weak and the frail, the poor and the sick, people who are "out of the mainstream" and don't know what life is all about. There is prayer, of course, in churches, at table, at dedications of bridges and inaugurations of public officials, but that is a matter of custom. And then there is prayer in operating rooms and at sickbeds. But that is just because of the desperate predicaments in which people find themselves. Mature, sophisticated persons, in full possession of their faculties, don't pray.

Or do they? People who pray, really pray, don't talk about it much. After you have looked into the matter carefully, you may be able to puzzle out who is really praying. In general, though, prayer is something of an underground. Is it because people who pray are too possessive about their experiences to share them? On the contrary, people who pray usually share their experiences generously. But on the whole they don't advertise their prayer-lives. Perhaps the energy that might be used in talk goes into prayer instead.

In order to find a person who prays, you have to look for clues: charitableness, good temper, patience, a fair ability to handle stress, resonance, openness to others. What happens to people who pray is that their inward life gradually takes over from their outward life. That is not to say that they are any less active. They may be competent lawyers, doctors, businessmen. But their hearts lie in the inner life and they are moved by that.

If, when you are beginning in prayer, you can identify one or more such people—at close range—you may be refreshed by their example. They will probably remind you—not by talk, but by example—that prayer is a matter of doing. This may help you to set all your awkwardness and excuses aside and simply begin.

Once you have begun, you will find yourself entering into a kind of life that seems very natural, as though you knew how to do it without being told; a life of following a path that is yours alone; a satisfying life that fills a need that was there all along, but somehow always an empty space before. As this happens you come to care less about "answers" to prayer and whether anything is "really" happening. Something *is* really happening, but it is entirely yours: a secret between you and God. Now you begin to sense why those who pray have some difficulty in talking about it.

It begins to seem as if the question of "answered prayers" is raised mainly by people who don't pray. It is as if they were saying, "What's in it for me? What can I get out of prayer?" This spirit is rather like that of certain bright students in college classes. They sit through the lecture trying to think of questions that will stump the professor. They are closing out the enlightenment they might receive by looking for a way to seize the role of authority figure for themselves. They are trying to second-guess God, to figure out how to get him to do it their way.

Petitions are, of course, a real and legitimate form of prayer. It is important in prayer to begin where you are, and if where you are is in a kind of sadness based on loss of certain promotions or preferments or human affections, it is better to tell it to God than to anyone. But one ought to try to move beyond the mentality of making requests and battering away at the indifference of heaven. The best thing to ask for in prayer is to be with the Lord. This prayer is a simple one and I have not heard of any instance in which it was not granted. In fact, once that prayer is granted, it may take a bit of getting used to. One's list of requests may need to be put aside for a while.

I think it is good at the beginning to have an uneventful prayer experience. It is a bit like the Stage Manager's advice to Emily in Thornton Wilder's play, *Our Town.* Emily, who had died, was to return to life for a day and wanted to choose a special occasion. The Stage Manager advised her to choose a day when nothing in particular was going on. For the beginner it is much the same. An "ordinary" time in the presence of God may be quite extraordinary. We are blessed if our prayer just flows along quietly:

> Yahweh, my heart has no lofty ambitions
>   My eyes do not look too high.
> I am not concerned with great affairs
>   or marvels beyond my scope.
> Enough for me to keep my soul tranquil
>   like a child in its mother's arms,
> as content as a child that has been weaned.
>
> Israel, rely on Yahweh,
>   now and for always![2]

Just the experience of setting the world aside for a brief span may be so exotic and unfamiliar that it pleases us enormously. We find ourselves able to listen to our own hearts, and they sound like thunder. We begin to get acquainted with ourselves. Slowly we begin to appreciate the good God sees in us:

Before the world was made, he chose us, chose us in Christ, to be holy and spotless, and to live through love in his presence, determining that we should become his. . . .[3]

One of the most appealing things about starting to pray is that we can please ourselves in prayer. It is like buying a pattern for embroidery or furnishing an empty room. We patch the fabric of our prayer together from the readings and devotions and images that please us most:

and you too have been stamped with the seal of the Holy Spirit of the Promise,

the pledge of our inheritance
which brings freedom for those whom God has taken for his own
to make his glory praised.[4]

Those who have complained loudly that the liturgy did not suit them, that the song leaders were off-key, and that the lectors mispronounced things have a chance in prayer to set everything straight. We can go to the Lord in prayer creatively, designing something to please ourselves and to praise him.

There is a kind of newness in the mere discovery that we can do this, that our prayer-lives can become our own invention rather than a burdensome duty laid upon us by someone else. Secretly, and with a kind of fresh enthusiasm, we begin to experiment with ways to pray. C. S. Lewis wrote of a practice (he thought it was his own device entirely) that he called festooning. Festooning, Lewis explained, was taking a familiar prayer, such as the Lord's prayer, and elaborating it, adding one's own intentions on at various points in the prayer until this elaboration became a ritual unto itself. For some, there is the pleasure of committing certain passages of Scripture to memory, a sort of mental scrapbook of private devotions. Somewhere along the line, a composition book is acquired, in which daily prayer experience is recorded. Perhaps the schedule is at once the most difficult and yet the most intriguing question: ought one to pray in the morning when one is freshest or sleepiest or at night when one has the most anxiety, more burdens to share with God?

To suggest that one may innovate in prayer is not to say that well-tried techniques should be avoided. There are ancient prayer-forms that seem to have the experience of the ages encoded in them. They haunt us with a sense of being at one with believers of the past and future. One learns to use the Psalms or the Jesus-Prayer, meditations that call up vivid scenes in the life of Christ. All these styles have value. Yet one should never become too entranced with method. Meister Eckhart is only one of the spiritual writers who offers us this caution:

You should not restrict yourself to any method, for God is not in any one kind of devotion, neither in this nor in that. Those who receive God thus, do him wrong. They receive the method and not God. . . .[5]

Method is important, but we must not introduce technology into prayer. A particular form may be attractive, but we should not think of any certain form as bringing results or success. Prayer will change us. It is not the method, however, that brings about the change.

People who pray make very strong claims for it. They say it helps them to get in touch with themselves, to solve problems, to experience healing of emotional hurts, to forgive and to aspire. When you pray, I have heard it said, you stop caring whether you live or die. (This I found hard to believe, but I believed in the person who said it.) All these claims arise from a belief that God's strength flows into us when we pray.

Ought we to pray for such reasons? Once we know them, it's hard to forget these beguiling incentives. But the best reason to pray is that God is really there. In praying, our unbelief gradually starts to melt. God moves smack into the middle of even an ordinary day. He is no longer someone we theorize about. He is someone we want to be near.

> I remember, and my soul
>   melts within me:
> I am on my way to the wonderful Tent,
>   to the house of God
> among cries of joy and praise
>   and an exultant throng.[6]

So we need delay no longer. It is time to begin. However stumbling or uncertain the beginning, it is worthwhile. And the beginning is more than the first stab or the first several stabs. Prayer is a matter of keeping at it. The rewards will come no other way. Thunderclaps and lightning flashes are very unlikely. It is well to start small and quietly. No need to tell one's friends and acquaintances. No need to plan heroic fasts or all-night vigils.

You should have it firm in your mind that prayer is neither to impress other people nor to impress God. It's not to be taken on with a mentality of success. The goal, in prayer, is to give oneself away. The Lord loves us—perhaps most of all—when we fail and try again.

NOTES

1. George Herbert, "Prayer (1)," *The Works of George Herbert*, ed. F. E. Hutchinson (Oxford: Clarendon Press, 1945), p. 51 (spelling and punctuation modernized).
2. Psalm 131. This and all other Scripture quotations are from the Jerusalem Bible.
3. Ephesians 1:4.
4. Ephesians 1:13–14.
5. Translation of Meister Eckhart by James M. Clark, quoted in Matthew Fox, *Breakthrough: Meister Eckhart's Creation Spirituality in New Translation* (New York: Doubleday Image, 1980), p. 209.
6. Psalm 42:4.

2. Yielding

The fact is that we are called to pray. It is not so much our doing as God's: a deep prompting within us that wells up without our meaning or intending it. It is the Lord's voice speaking, calling us to him, yet sometimes at first so quietly that without stopping to listen, we don't hear it. But the call is real. The Lord is there.

It is the call of him who made us and meant from the beginning that we should belong to him. He shaped us, formed us, and with a special destiny in mind. That is the secret we are longing to know—the reason for our being. It is a secret known only to him, one he will tell us when we come near to him in prayer.

He is the one who can tell us the reason for our existence, our place in the scheme of things, our real identity. It is an identity we can't discover for ourselves, that others can't discover in us—the mystery of who we really are. How we have chased around the world for answers to that riddle, looked in the eyes of others for some hint, some clue, hunted in the multiple worlds of pleasure and experience and self-fulfillment for some glimpse, some revelation, some wisdom, some authority to tell us our right name and our true destination.

But there was, and is, only One who can tell us this: the Lord himself. And he wants to tell us, he has made us to know our reason for being and to be led by it. But it is a secret he will entrust to us only when we ask, and then in his own way and his own time. He will whisper it to us not in the mad rush and fever of our striving and our fierce determination to be someone, but rather when we are content to rest in him, to put ourselves into his keeping, into his hands. Most delightfully of all, it is a secret he will tell us slowly and sweetly, when we are willing to spend time with him: time with him who is beyond all time.

I myself taught Ephraim to walk,
I took them in my arms;
yet they have not understood that I was the one looking after them.
I led them with reins of kindness,
with leading strings of love.
I was like someone who lifts an infant close against his cheek;
stooping down to him I gave him his food.[1]

So it seems the most important starting point for prayer is yielding: laying down our defenses, taking off masks, recognizing that God has already called us and is already waiting for us to come to him. Yielding is putting aside our self-importance, our cares and schedules and undertakings, in order, very simply, to be with God. It is the yielding up of everything that keeps us from the Lord, letting go of anxiety and restlessness. It is the gift to him of time, the only coin we have to spend: the gift of ourselves, one we find all too difficult to give.

How hard is it to set aside time each day to be with God? Sometimes it seems impossible. Yet how many minutes do we spend each day in conversation with people we care about little, who care about us not at all? How much time do we spend in searching for more effective ways to manage our time so that we can spend more time becoming effective? How much time do we spend in anxious fretting and striving about things that are beyond our control?

Can any of you, for all his worrying, add a single cubit to his span of life? If the smallest things, therefore, are outside your control, why worry about the rest?[2]

Even one minute a day, sixty seconds by the clock, is more than we can sometimes find for prayer. With all our managing, we cannot manage time for this. Yet that very minute with the Lord can be a step into eternity, a passageway into the kingdom.

No; set your hearts on his kingdom, and these other things will be given you as well. There is no need to be afraid . . . for it has pleased your Father to give you the kingdom.[3]

Is it possible, with all our striving, that we can't find so much as a minute a day for the Lord? Would five minutes be completely out of the question? Is it possible that we have allowed ourselves to slide so far, to be so distant from the spirit of prayer, that we suppose five minutes would not do, because first we would need fifteen minutes to unwind, to prepare? Suddenly we know that the barrier is not time at all, not the pressure of events, not the many demands on our talents and our charity, but an obstacle within ourselves, a stubbornness that will not yield to Him.

Yielding is bending. It is hard to think about, easier to do. Once it is done, it is a loosing of every bond that holds us in the here and now, a step into the glorious freedom of the sons and daughters of God.

It is step into reality, a movement through the darkling glass that keeps us from our Lord: a passage into freedom, into a childhood of the spirit where identity is known not by hints or explanations, but by a light that falls on us from Him.

> God, you are my God, I am seeking you,
> my soul is thirsting for you,
> my flesh is longing for you.
> a land parched, weary and waterless;
> I long to gaze on you in the Sanctuary
> and to see your power and glory.[4]

Some people say they don't know how to pray. What they want is to be told the correct way: surefire forms of words, reliable prayers and recitations, meditations and exercises. These are good ways to prayer. But they are only means and instruments. They are systems for coming to quiet, methods often meant to slow us down and make it possible for us to hear God's voice, to sense his presence. They are not yet prayer itself. They are paths toward prayer, the stepping stones from our furious activity and movement into his life, his being.

It is there that the Lord teaches us to pray. When we begin to pray, he prays in us; it is his power and grace that help us pray, till we don't know where we leave off and he begins. We yield. And when that yielding comes, we find that all the prayers made up since time began are swept aside and something new occurs. Something happens now for the first time between the Lord and us, something springs from his reality and our response, from his identity and ours in him. We do not speak. He speaks. We do not ask. He asks. He is the music that fills the universe, and we—with our first fumbling steps—now catch the rhythm of the dance.

> Your love is better than life itself,
> my lips will recite your praise;
> all my life I will bless you,
> in your name lift up my hands;
> my soul will feast most richly,
> on my lips a song of joy and, in my mouth, praise.[5]

There are no words now, for our prayer moves beyond words. And yet there is a to-and-fro about it. He is calling us and we are following. He is surprising us—now here, now there—and we are chasing him. Time stops, the music of his presence moves us, leads us in ways we had not dreamed of, shows us gleams of an existence we hardly guessed at. We are children now, chasing the kingdom, stepping free of where we were and who we were, into new selves, made in his image and likeness, selves of his making, meant for heaven and for him.

Now we exist with God. In him we live and move. That is so always, the reality of our existence even when we do not sense it. But now we know it to be true; in prayer, the truth of it is suddenly made clear. His presence overshadows us. His power is 'round about us. In prayer, we know, just for a time, that he who hung the stars and moves the planets made us, too—made us for his own reason, called us into being, holds us each instant in existence, and calls us to reality in him.

How can we know that, except by grace: God in us, making known a mystery beyond speech, a knowing deeper than all ordinary knowing? It is as though our lives were lit up from within and some revelation—not breaking through like miracles, but some entirely natural disclosure meant for each one alone—were being whispered in the depths of the heart.

> Do not be afraid, for I have redeemed you;
> I have called you by your name, you are mine.
> Should you pass through the sea, I will be with you;
> or through rivers, they will not swallow you up.
> Should you walk through fire, you will not be scorched
> and the flames will not burn you.[6]

This is the knowing that comes from yielding, believing that the word of God is true and will be finally made plain in us, opening up to that astounding possibility without reserve and without hesitation.

> On my bed I think of you,
> I meditate on you all night long,
> for you have always helped me.
> I sing for joy in the shadow of your wings;
> my soul clings close to you,
> your right hand supports me.[7]

We know him because we yield to him—opening up every crevice of ourselves where anger, fear, and doubt are hidden—yielding up imagination most of all, to be transformed by him into a means of grace, a way of entering the kingdom.

> Can it argue with the man who fashioned it,
> one vessel among earthen vessels?
> Does the clay say to its fashioner, "What are you making?"
> does the thing he shaped say, "You have no skill"? . . .
> Is it for you to question me . . .
> and to dictate to me what my hands should do?[8]

Imagination is a way to prayer. For some, it may be possible to move at once into that nothingness the mystics speak of. But for many ordinary Christians, it is first necessary to envision God and to envision one who can be spoken to:

> Oh, come to the water all you who are thirsty;
> though you have no money, come! . . .
>
> Pay attention, come to me;
> listen, and your soul will live.[9]

For some, the many images presented by the Faith already, the great paintings and imagery of old religious art are sufficient. But others find these images are stumbling blocks. They hold us back from prayer. Then it becomes important—imperative—to image God in our own minds so that we can come near to him. In fact, he wills us to do that, to set aside false images of faith, see what is troubling in them, and move toward our most helpful image of the Lord, the one that is both awe and invitation, the God we seek behind all images:

> Seek Yahweh while he is still to be found,
> call to him while he is still near . . .
> to our God who is rich and forgiving;
> for my thoughts are not your thoughts,
> my ways not your ways—it is Yahweh who speaks.[10]

For me, the Scriptures were from childhood a way to pray. I learned some psalms by heart, and in them I found images that told me of the Lord's concern for me, his power and protection. They told me of his justice, too: that all the flaws and failings of humanity were known, wickedness and deception among us could not deceive him, all things would somehow be made right again. That image of God in Scripture, God as a rock, God as a deliverer, God loving us and choosing us and taking us to him because of what he loves in us, throwing our sins behind his back, forgetting our transgressions—that image is enduring and powerful for me. So it was from that childlike vision that again, in later life, I drew my vision of the Lord, now knowing, more profoundly than I had, the fact of sin, the strength of human envy, greed, self-righteousness, the possibility of cruelty and anger, the likelihood of degradation and pain.

As an adult, I earned the possibility of blaming everything on God—something that, as a child, I had not known. As a child, I had seen in God all goodness. If something went wrong, I was to blame. Now as an adult, I learned that one could blame all the wrongs on God and punish him for his transgressions.

To learn to pray again I had to learn to set aside both childish and adult misconceptions in my image of God. I had to start again, from knowing him to be the God who made the universe, and made us, too; the God who overlooked our waywardness and disobedience; the God who went so far as to become what we are, to take on our humanity, in order to show us the reality of his design for us, our destiny, the overcoming power of his love. I had to use all my creative skill—a gift from him, I now remembered—to sketch an image in my mind of the real God, the living God who is and acts, who holds existence in his hand and holds us close to him.

I had to learn to see my Savior as he is: entirely man, entirely God, not one more than another, contradicting rationality by his reality: pouring himself out for us on the cross and raising us with him.

I had to learn to see my Lord acting in history and time: closer to me than my own heartbeat and as close as that to every human being; acting in me and changing me to bring me closer to my destiny; acting in others, showing himself to me through them. I had to see my Lord as present here and now and, most of all, as present in my prayer.

> Yahweh is tender and compassionate,
> slow to anger, most loving . . .
> he never treats us, never punishes us,
> as our guilt and our sins deserve.[11]

But what resources were given to me to do this! I had the overflowing power of the Scriptures, the riches of the church, God imaged in the Eucharist and in the saints. I had God's image in holy people that I knew, in those I loved, and in the wonder of the creative spirit of humanity, the miracle of thought itself, the very fact of my imagination transcending place and time.

Yet without yielding—the willingness to image God and see

him where he is most willing to reveal himself—I could not know him. It was my willingness, my openness, my yielding, my free consent to dream of God by that imaginative power he had given me—it was my yes that was required. That same imaginative power with which I could draw near to him could also be exerted to exclude him from everything I did and saw.

"Put yourself in the presence of God," Francis de Sales advised. For C. S. Lewis, the God he could approach in prayer was always a "bright blur" within his consciousness, a power too great ever to be quite captured in a picture designed by him or us. And so it is with each of us. We do not make God in our image and, if we are wise, we refuse to do so. All images of our own making must be rejected in the end as false or incomplete, inadequate to capture the Lord of all creation. And yet we seek him everywhere and sometimes find, even in naked thought, the image—as Merton found, while reading philosophy, the God who is "pure act, immutable"—the God who speaks to our imagination.

> To whom could you liken God?
> What image could you contrive of Him? . . .
> and who could be my equal? says the Holy One.[12]

When we find him, wherever and whenever we do, we do not need to will ourselves to pray. Prayer then springs up, a sudden fountain of wonder and of praise.

But always, there must be yielding: yielding to God in us, in others, in himself. A willingness to bend the knee and know that he has made us, not we ourselves, and most of all, that he has made us to be loved by him and that he loves us, always and most of all.

NOTES

1. Hosea 11:3–4.
2. Luke 12:25–26.

3. Luke 12:31–32.
4. Psalm 63:1–2.
5. Psalm 63:3–4.
6. Isaiah 43:1–2.
7. Psalm 63:6–8.
8. Isaiah 45:9.
9. Isaiah 55:1, 3.
10. Isaiah 55:6–8.
11. Psalm 103:8–9.
12. Isaiah 40:18, 25.

3. Darkness

I want to speak now of darkness, as it were, out of sequence, and partly to make the very point that there is no sequence in prayer.

That is to say, there is no sequence we can count on or anticipate in advance. Yes, one prayer experience does follow another, and without question, God has something in mind for us, however little we can follow the thread. But sequence—in the sense of proper sequence, a scheme by which one moves from one stage to the next, or upwards, from level to level of achievement—is a notion we ought to let go of as best we can. Looking for a given scheme, measuring ourselves by it, is a self-regarding, self-conscious practice. It sets limitations on our prayer, sets us up for disappointment, creates false expectancies, arouses a success mentality by which we constantly ask to know whether we have arrived. We want to know whether God is finding us worthy for this or that prayer experience. Not only do we wait for and long for consolations. We even wait for darkness as a sign that God is preparing us for a difficult call.

Even as I wrote in the last chapter about the sweetness that comes sometimes in prayer, the rhythm that seems to be not our rhythm, but God's, I remembered that it is not always so, for anyone. Even to write of consolations is to set too high a value on sweetness. Sweetness is incidental. It is not the thing itself. Nor is darkness the thing. Yet darkness is a definite experience of prayer, surely not to be sought, almost impossible to flee from.

What if nothing happens when I pray? And what if the nothing that happens is not a very special sort of nothing, one that I could dramatize as a dark night, but instead the completely vacuous and even boring nothing in which I cannot make any headway at all, in which it seems I have taken a wrong turn, or lost the map entirely? What if the clarity of yesterday's prayer now seems like a made-up story and nothing more than delusion?

Well, that is darkness of a sort. When it comes, it is precisely the nothing happening that is in fact something happening. Something is happening. We are being asked to hold on by faith and to go on praying when we have no sense of progress or momentum at all. The something is that we are being asked to be ordinary in prayer.

Some of the great spiritual writers have spoken of the unspeakable pleasures and consolations that come to beginners, suggesting that these are given to us because we are infants in prayer, needing comfort and sweetness. The Lord gives us these pleasures to encourage us.

But there is no map. Even the beginner may start by experiencing "nothing in particular" in prayer. He or she may be like James Thurber who, try as he would, could not see what everyone else in the science lab could see through the microscope. The beginner ought not to begin by expecting beginner's pleasures. If the beginner finds darkness, he or she should not start by counting on the spiritual life of John of the Cross. Each person is given only what God intends for that moment at that precise intersection between God and the individual made possible by prayer.

How tempting to compare and contrast! How humanly we wish to do well with God by following some prescribed path! Even that aspect of our humanity must simply be accepted for what it is, laughed at, and forgotten about. There is no sense accusing ourselves of being human.

But if prayer is so indescribably particular, how then write about or describe it at all? With some cautions and reservations, it is still worth doing. However much I travel the path on my own timetable, known only slightly to me and entirely to God, there is nonetheless a commonality in the experience. When I come to a given place in the road, I sense that many have passed there before.

Darkness is worth describing simply because it is so unlike what we expect. It is not consolation disguised as desolation. It does not meet our expectation that darkness will blaze with intensity. Darkness is not, as we had thought, just light turned inside out.

Darkness, when it comes, is not *like* anything. It is itself. And just what we might expect from God, a surprise.

The surprise is partly that the Lord is bound by no sequence of anyone's devising, and therefore we may find darkness at the beginning, middle, or end, or sprinkled anywhere along the way. We may go in and out of it as we do with rainstorms on a highway. Even that patchiness contradicts our expectation of clear shape and meaning.

But what is more important than our inability to control or predict darkness is the sudden understanding we have that this darkness, which comes at the beginning, or in the middle, or whenever, is the very same darkness as any other darkness. It is not different in character from the darkness that the saints and mystics have told us to expect at the heights of prayer.

When it comes, it does not have the character of something, but of nothing. One does not seem to arrive anywhere, but nowhere. There is a muddledness about it. It feels so in-between. The music of our prayer is gone, but the silence that follows is not sharp with meaning or confrontation. It is a mere absence of sound. There is no drama in our darkness. We are not doomed or lost in space in a way that permits us to become the center of everything by our very alienation. Instead, the nowhere of our darkness is an indeterminate state, without conclusion or resolution. There is nothing decisive to react to or act upon. It is like long afternoons in childhood when it is raining and there is nothing special to do. Like waiting for something without being able to be anxious for an outcome, because nothing particular is at issue. The waiting does not prove anything one way or the other. Darkness shows us the unresolvability of things, opens up the possibility of being permanently at loose ends. At the same time, there is no permanence in it, nothing so well defined. It is a mystery, but one that does not evoke awe and reverence. Instead, this intermediate, free-floating state cannot even be called surrender, for surrender is at least a depth, a crisis stage, a turning point. And darkness is not all at once. It is sustained. It has extension, but no visible shape. It seems to be going on forever. Yet our faith is still present and we know God is there. He is there, but the bush does not burn. Nothing breaks through or intervenes. The sky is the same color as if God were not . . . *as if.* We know God is present, but we have no sense of him.

Darkness is an unsensation.

It is neither bitter nor sweet.

It is not hot or cold, not wet or dry. We are not swallowed up in it. We are simply there, in a sort of vacuum that is not void because everything goes on as before, in a sequence of utterly humdrum and meaningless events. The day-to-dayness continues and cannot be stemmed. If we were not believers, we would despair. Such ordinariness calls for something to break the tedium, seeking a high, pulling wings off dragonflies, setting something on fire to watch it burn. But we keep on as before.

Yet notice one thing. This darkness is never so dark that we can say for sure we have been *given darkness,* by which we might have the assurance of knowing that darkness is part of some scheme for our improvement, a riddle to be guessed so we can go to the next part of the game. Such darkness would be mere pretending. But our God is not playing tricks. He doesn't set traps like some Olympian practical joker of a deity. Instead, the darkness he sends is so real that you can't see your hand in front of your face. So real that you can't suspect it has been sent as a gift. So real that you can't even sense it as a test or as a trial.

All we can do with this darkness is bear it, live it, accept and endure it. And draw a box around it with the crayon of our prayer.

We can't break through it, disperse it, or go around it. The way lies straight ahead. And if we run away from it—by not praying, for instance—we find that in our not-praying we bring it with us, like that moon which follows us along a dark highway, merely shifting position when we turn a curve.

> An enemy who hounds me
> to crush me into the dust,
> forces me to dwell in darkness
> like the dead of long ago;
> my spirit fails me
> and my heart is full of fear.[1]

I remember clearly (and any day it might come again) the terrible reluctance to start praying on the chance that the first thing I would find is a wall. And the wall, I knew, would not be a wall at which I was to stop, but one I was expected to walk through.

And when one asks the Lord in prayer about the wall, asking him to take the wall away, the answer is simply that the wall exists in order for us to walk through it.

But the remarkable thing is that we do. We walk into and through the wall in a way that is beyond comprehension. This impossible thing that is quite beyond us and that we nevertheless are able to do shows us both an inevitability and an incomprehensible overturning of the systematic order of things. It is the what-we-can't-do-under-any-circumstances that is nevertheless to be done.

Darkness comes to deepen our prayer and to strengthen us. But God does this not all at once and not by seeming to. This experience is different from any other, akin to pain but not like pain because it has no sharp edges. It is the bleakness of grief without any object of grief. No one has died, nothing is lost to us, except perhaps a vision we once had and were clinging to, instead of God himself. Now God, still present, takes his presence from us and we experience nothing. And we live with that.

Running away from darkness is very human. I suspect it must be commonplace. Because we expected so much peace and hopefulness from prayer, we feel momentarily cheated, stung—but something has been taken away that was not ours to begin with. We run from this unfairness, but there is nowhere to run.

It would be well now to remember, if we can do it without too much spiritual ambition, that the dark way was the way in which the Father led the Son.

Even in Gethsemane he did not run. He wanted to. He asked for the cup to pass. But he did not run.

We are, however, much more like Peter. It doesn't seem right to us for the story to be told this way. We ask for a different, happier ending.

What if the Father had given Peter his pleasant earthly resolution? The story we are part of will surely be told better than we know how.

In Gethsemane, in the prison, at the interrogation, in the trial, on the Jerusalem streets, up Calvary's hill, must not it have seemed to Christ that the drama was oppressive, acted out by fools, that the lines being spoken were a crazy distortion of the way things ought to be?

Or if, as our faith tells us, he knew all along it must be so, saw in advance how the plot must fall, was it not then a heightened consciousness for him—a darkness in reverse—to know what he knew and what we did not understand, to be himself and us all at once? Yet he did not run.

Though we know by faith that his resolve would not flag and his trust would not be shaken, isn't it also clear that he has lived out our darkness for us as he has lived out our death? And has shown us the way to cling now to a resurrection we sense as ours but don't yet possess?

Trust and faith are the only companions for darkness, a walk that doesn't feel like a journey because there is no sense of going anywhere.

It can come at any moment, remain any length of time, and can't be second-guessed. But it can be lived through and prayed through.

One thing, perhaps, can make it bearable, though it may seem like mockery to some: it is not general but particular darkness. My darkness is my own.

It is not beyond my powers of acceptance, however it might seem to stretch me beyond my limits. And darkness is a call.

It is not like those calls in which decisive life-choices are before us.

But it is, even so, the call to leave everything and follow him, the call to drop nets and leave wife and children and parents and every earthly thing.

The call is all the harder when we are asked to leave them without them, to be detached, as it were, in place, without budging an inch from home.

Darkness calls us to fast by washing our faces and going on as though nothing were happening, to fast from fasting itself, from anything with sharp edges and neat borders meant to convince us we are getting somewhere.

Darkness calls us to detachment from somewhere and the need to arrive there.

> My son, if you aspire to serve the Lord,
>   prepare yourself for an ordeal.
> Be sincere of heart, be steadfast,
>   and do not be alarmed when disaster comes.
> Cling to him and do not leave him,
>   so that you may be honored at the end of your days.
> Whatever happens to you, accept it,
>   and in the uncertainties of your humble state, be patient,
> since gold is tested in the fire,
>   and chosen men in the furnace of humiliation.[2]

Darkness is one foot in front of another. It is "most men lead lives of quiet desperation" lived in trust. It is doing what comes to hand without feeling or seeing the grace by which it is to be done.

Do you remember, when we were children, how we could not feel ourselves growing? The change in us could not be sensed until someone else insisted we had become taller and measured us against himself.

Darkness, then, is that growth that comes in silence and by remaining perfectly still.

We may be traveling at the speed of light, but it seems we are not moving at all.

In darkness it is worth trying Newman's prayer:

God has created me
to do Him some definite service
He has committed some work to me
which He has not committed to another

I have my mission
I may never know it in this life
But I shall be told it in the next

I am a link in a chain
A bond of connection between persons
He has not created me for naught
I shall do good—I shall do His work
I shall be an angel of peace
A preacher of truth in my own place
While not intending it
If I do but keep His commandments.

Therefore I will trust Him
whatever I am, I can never be thrown away
If I am in sickness, my sickness may serve Him
In perplexity, my perplexity may serve Him
If I am in sorrow, my sorrow may serve Him

He does nothing in vain
He knows what He is about
He may take away my friends
He may throw me among strangers
He may make me feel desolate
make my spirits sink
hide my future from me—still
He knows what He is about.[3]

Newman's affirmation is a sure way to go in darkness. It leads us, without signposts or milestones, towards the height and depth and width of Christ's own prayer.

The goal, in darkness, is not to whimper about it, but to live it, while it lasts, as deeply as any other gift God gives us in experience. One day, without knowing how or why, something has lifted. The darkness has simply gone away.

NOTES

1. Psalm 143:3–4
2. Ecclesiasticus 2:1–5
3. Prayer attributed to John Henry Newman.

4. Transparency

Transparency is more than a chosen figure for the way we experience gifts and growth in prayer. It is not so much a metaphor as a naming of the comprehension and vision that comes about in us as we continue to pray.

I do not offer it as a guaranteed or even a likely effect. If one looks for a list of what to expect as the fruit or effect of the spirit within us, it would be well to look to Scripture itself, where all the best and most reliable promises are.

In Galatians 5, we learn that the fruits of the spirit are charity, joy, peace, patience, benignity, goodness, longanimity, mildness, faith, modesty, continency, and chastity. In Isaiah 11, we hear of the gifts of the spirit: wisdom, understanding, counsel, knowledge, fortitude, piety, fear of the Lord.

I recall once, to encourage myself in prayer, having written those promises down on a three-by-five card. I believed then, and believe now, that these fruits and gifts do follow those who believe.

It is not my intent, however, to "translate" from scriptural authority, but to begin from experience itself. Those desirable gifts may indeed follow upon our prayer and dedication to the Lord, but when they do, we ourselves rarely sense them. Others may perceive them to be true of us; we can see them in others, not in ourselves.

Transparency is one of the effects of prayer from the point of view of the one who prays. It is that growing clarity which happens, almost in spite of us, the more we give ourselves to prayer. It is a kind of immediacy, an insight—a sense of being able to enter into "things," into experience, more deeply and in a way we had not entirely anticipated. It is a grasping of existence itself, possessing it, in an unaccountably different way. Yet by this I do not mean a peak experience in the sense of being at the heights. Instead, I mean a sense that day-to-day existence, events, persons, actions, the things that are already ours seem to be more ours than before, more open, more available to us.

> Where could I go to escape your spirit?
> Where could I flee from your presence?
> If I climb the heavens, you are there,
> there, too, if I lie in Sheol.[1]

Is there an inherent contradiction in the darkness I described before and the transparency I am describing now? Surely light and darkness cannot coexist in the same individual at the same time! It is true that darkness and transparency may be experienced as alternatives. But they are not opposites. By a kind of paradox they may sometimes be aspects of the same moment, a duality that occurs within us when we pray—perhaps even because we pray.

> If I asked darkness to cover me,
> and light to become night around me,
> that darkness would not be dark to you,
> night would be as light as day.[2]

Transparency is neither light nor illumination, precisely. It is that experience of going beyond ourselves and our limitations while at the same time being conscious of the definition of ourselves. It is the grasp of reality that comes about not from an effort to master circumstance, but instead from a full admission of our powerlessness and our inability to comprehend events. The more we admit what we are and are not, the more we come to know how little we can accomplish and control, how inadequate our formulas are to express reality, the more we encounter the edges of the world falling away from us, the ships, once seen at a distance, now disappearing over the rim of the world, the more we know the arc of our own vision and are conscious of the boundedness of our experience—with the years, becoming more and more defined by our humanity—the more, by an inexplicable paradox and mystery, we see. The universe, everything is made known to us, given to us by God, lit up from within. And the more this happens, the more we sense the wonder: that which we could not be for ourselves, God is for us.

> If I flew to the point of sunrise,
> or westward across the sea,
> your hand would still be guiding me,
> your right hand holding me.[3]

Sometimes this experience of transparency is an experience of particularity. This one moment that I am now experiencing, this rainstorm in which I am being soaked and drenched, this feeling of mushiness in my shoes, this joke, these tears, this catness of a cat jumping up into a windowsill, this ability to know that the air is damp and that the leaves of the caladium plant, deep red at the center, green at the edge, are shining with wetness, through the garden window, just *there*, that very ability to experience the *thisness* of things, is a glimpse of the real. God is not so much everywhere, or in heaven, as in this one moment, and I am, like George Herbert, there with him:

> Whether I fly with angels, fall with dust,
> Thy hands made both, and I am there:
> Thy power and love, my love and trust
> Make one place everywhere.[4]

And this experience of God-in-the-particular-person, God-in-the-moment, or God-in-the-event is everything that I am and everything that God is in a single glimpse. A leaf, the root of a tree, the dimeness of a coin glinting in the palm of my hand . . . (this very dime, no other!)—thisness floods us with conclusiveness. Instant on instant, one following another, is Yahweh saying, I am.

Against that particularity which reveals a meaning in every instant, some contrariness in us sets up a constant wail, arguing for the subjectivity of our perception, for the possibility of projection—us putting the meaning in, rather than God being in the moment for us. But when we pray, and are living with prayer, drenched and soaked in it, those considerations are gnats and mosquitoes to us, merely to be batted at and brushed away. The dogs yelp, but the caravan of our movement into God pushes on.

Sometimes this transparency is experienced almost as a capacity to read hearts: to know the thoughts of others, even their hatreds, without being told.

But I say this to you: love your enemies and pray for those who persecute you.[5]

Not only from the eyes and the body language do we know it, but by some immediacy of vision, some seeing, which seems to come not from anything we do, but to be pure gift.

[A] full measure, pressed down, shaken together, running over, will be poured into your lap.[6]

And it is this seeing that makes it possible at last to love the ones who hate us and whom we, too, have provocation to hate. In the comprehension of our seeing, we go past the outer image of the person to the inner image that God created, an identity imperfectly seen, perhaps, but plain enough to compel our charity and our love.

> You will seek but never find them,
> these enemies of yours.
> They shall be destroyed and brought to nothing,
> those who made war on you.[7]

This transparency I speak of, this seeing, is not so much something that takes place when we pray, or within our prayer, as outside of our prayer and because we pray. It is a residue of prayer: prayer carried with us into the rest of life.

This change in ourselves also lets us see Christ in the pain of events, in the distress and despair of others, in the homeless drifters, in their faces and bodies ravaged by alcohol, their destitution, their hopelessness. Because of transparency, we can love them, experience their pain with them, and be moved towards them to help, to attend, to do for them what we can, and to take them generously into our prayer.

That transparency makes us able to feel our identity with those in need, even to the point of saying, "I love you" to the panhandler who meets us in the street and begs what little of our substance we have to spare.

Take the plank out of your own eye first, and then you will see clearly enough to take the splinter out of your brother's eye.[8]

This comprehension also begins to help us confront our own defeats with equanimity, lets us distance from our own anxiety and call it by its rightful name. It is the seeing that lets us walk ahead on a path that is not plain, where the destination is entirely hidden, but with a constant sense that God himself is both at the destination and along the way.

It is the possibility—not instantly, but without much lapse of time—of understanding our own yearning, our constant restless longing, our will to have-what-we-have-not, to reshape reality to some other end, that desire for conclusiveness and resolution, which is most intensely with us in darkness, but is in fact an everpresent condition of our existence. To recognize that yearning is to diminish for a moment the spell in which it holds us and to move beyond it, accepting it as a given of our humanity.

Transparency is a passage into the fullness that makes us want to fast. It is an understanding that not-tasting is better than tasting, closer to the sum and substance of reality. It is a comprehension of the falsity of sampling experience as a way to fulfillment, even a questioning of the very notion of fulfillment—an understanding that doing without pleasure, the emptiness that makes itself empty for God, so sharply different from fasting to seek the experience of fasting, is a deeper experience of truth than the constant rush to plunge into and taste things, if only to say we have done so.

Because of this, the very transparency that moves us close to others sharply separates us from some. Seeing what we see, we feel a distance from those conversations that are accumulations of what-I-did, and where-I've-been, and who-I-know, and what-I-own. The seeing that sees through these things makes it harder to enter into dialogue with those who live by things. Transparency sees some modes of life crumbling to ashes before our very eyes. We can no longer live for the dreams that some are moved by. Silence, stillness, a dreaming within us calls us to a depth that cannot even be spoken of. So our clarity loosens and disentangles us from some kinds of amusement and conversation. As we become more aware of an inner reality, some kinds of business and occupation seem totally beside the point. We no longer live, as we once did, for doing. Now what we burn for is stillness. We cultivate not the pleasures of going and coming and doing, but the peacefulness and abandonment of not-doing, which is an experience of the wonder of God. It is the clarity that knows less is more, the realization that we need not carve our mark upon existence, so much as we need to let it carve its mark upon us.

Chastity, continence, mildness, modesty, patience, longanimity—all these not-as-the-world-sees kinds of goodness flow spontaneously from the clarity of vision given to us. Even to those very persons with whom we cannot share that vision, our charity flows irrepressibly out, a kindness that flows from the unveiling of experience going on in us minute to minute and day to day.

The apparent facts of existence—the sadness, the sorrow, the anxiety, the emptiness, the pain—seem now actually to call us to contemplation of Christ within events. Within events themselves, by this way of seeing, we know Christ changing the monstrous observable facts into an image of himself.

Transparency overturns our notion of God as there-and-later, while everything else is here-and-now. But, through prayer, we begin to see God as here-and-now within and during and as part of what-seems-not-to-be-God's that is also here-and-now.

This happens not because we think it, imagine it, project it, but because we live it by prayer that puts us into the heart of things as they actually are.

Out of his infinite glory, may he give you the power through his Spirit for your hidden self to grow strong, so that Christ may live in your hearts through faith, and then, planted in love and built on love, you will with all the saints have strength to grasp the breadth and the length, the height and the depth. . . .[9]

Perhaps the most noticeable thing about transparency, a corollary of it, is our becoming very open to love. More and more we are vulnerable to darts—a dart from ambush, some totally unexpected love striking through to the center of our being—and the dart that pierces so suddenly and surprisingly is not sent by another person to us, but in behalf of another person, by Christ himself.

NOTES

1. Psalm 139:7–8.
2. Psalm 139:11–12.
3. Psalm 139:9–10.
4. George Herbert, "The Temper (1)," *The Works of George Herbert*, ed. F. E. Hutchinson (Oxford: Clarendon Press, 1945), p. 55 (spelling and punctuation modernized).
5. Matthew 5:44–45.
6. Luke 6:38.
7. Isaiah 41:12.
8. Luke 7:5.
9. Ephesians 3:16–19.

5. Hoops of Steel

How amazing it is to love and be loved. How unlike what we supposed it to be! How astonishing that this capacity grows more so with each love, so that we feel, even in the pain of a declining love, the deepening possibilities of loving again. All the while we resist and draw back from love—mindful of the mingled pleasure and pain of it, the vulnerability, the surrender, the helplessness in the hands of another person—we also run headlong into it with joy, careless as children who experience intense affection for the first time.

Amazing, too, that the life of the spirit in us makes it possible to love God first in himself, and then in another person, and that he definitely and without question sends himself to us in a person he has made. What a sharp sense of grace there is in discovering a person so made for us, so shaped that it seems that person was destined for us from birth, whose mind is open to us as though we together were thinking the same thoughts at the same moment, so that the very fact of this person is for us a proof of the existence of God.

Jonathan's soul became closely bound to David's and Jonathan came to love him as his own soul. . . . He took off the cloak he was wearing and gave it to David, and his armor too, even his bow and his belt.[1]

And at the same time, how much, in the like-mindedness of the other person we also sense a difference. The very kindredness of that person is a reminder of otherness, the exquisiteness of that person's being entirely herself or himself so that in all creation there is no one else like this. In knowing the other person, we experience, as though for the first time and in a way that seems entirely new, the "old" recognition: God exists and has made me for himself. He knows my inward self, the me that can never disclose myself to anyone but him, knows me so well that he has made a companion just for me.

The love of the spirit is this very keen discovery: this setting out in search of some precious prize with a high heart and the pleasure of companionship. This is the adventure of having a partner in prayer.

Does it still happen that friends of the heart can be close as Paul and Timothy?

Night and day I thank God . . . and always I remember you in my prayers; I remember your tears and long to see you again to complete my happiness. . . . This is why I am reminding you now to fan into a flame the gift that God gave you when I laid my hands on you.[2]

Don't ask me where such a friend can be found. It is hardly a question of finding at all, for nothing we do can ever accomplish it. To "find" a spiritual friend is truly to be found, to be chased down, smoked out of one's hiding place in the corner of existence and brought into the center, swept into the blazing presence of God.

But—perhaps this is just a description of merely human love? An experience so keen and so temporal, so fleeting that there is no way to take hold of it except to call it divine?

"Ordinary" human love—which is, of course, never ordinary—is all these things I have described. But the love of two human beings for each other which is charged with the presence of God is all that and more.

There is a hush in it, a stillness, a wonder, that drives us to prayer and into prayer, drives us deeper into God and towards heaven. This is a friendship that is never consummated or possessed, fully, except in the context of God, with a consciousness of God dwelling in the other person, and in ourselves, and in the space between us, a space that seems to be continually dwindling because it soon becomes impossible to know where I leave off and the other person begins.

In this one sort of experience, the yearning that seemed a constant of our existence here and now is somehow eased and we feel we have come home.

Prayer, it seems, disposes us to friendship, in that it more and more lays us open to experience from any source, makes us sensitive to every aspect of existence, every leaf, every ray of light, every hurt, every sorrow, every pain.

And because of prayer, it somehow becomes possible to take up each friendship into ourselves and make it part of our own way of loving, so that the next experience of a loving heart becomes an expansion not only of ourselves, but of all the loves we already bear within us, enriching all those affections already embedded in our hearts.

Because we love this new person, we love more intensely, and more freshly, and with a new immediacy those whom we already love. Love squares and cubes in us. It is the overflowing pitcher, the bottomless cup.

How can I describe the simple tenderness that comes to exist reciprocally between two people who love God in himself and in each other—in the very same way?

That tenderness doesn't come all at once, but is wrested, gradually, from the first intensity of love that seemed, truly, like a descent of the divine into us, a flame that was too much to bear.

If it were not for this transformation of passion into tenderness that comes with time and with fidelity to God himself, undoubtedly such friendship would flame out, leaving us scorched, exhausted, in despair.

But the intensity, by our very faithfulness and constancy to God's call, is stretched out, elongated, shaped into a gentle perseverance in love that can stand the day-to-day reality.

And this tenderness that is an evenness in our loving, a sense of being loved without flirtation, dalliance, little exchanges of words and reassurances, this love made into prayer and transformed by prayer is, I like to think, the friendship of the saints, in heaven and on earth.

To understand this love, it is only necessary to compare it with the sort of human love most of us have experienced at some time or other: that love which becomes a way of hiding one's feelings, one's inner self, from another person, a kind of game-playing in which cards are held close to the vest, and with the thought, I-will-not-let-you-know-how-much-I-love-you-lest-you-have-power-over-me.

To love another person in God is very different from that. To love in Christ, to move and have one's being in him, is to magnify another person, to strengthen that person, to take the other's fears and concerns as our own, to exchange places and to love her or him not only as ourselves, but even (so we sense it) more than we love ourselves.

It is the love that Aelred speaks of in his treatise on spiritual friendship:

And so in friendship are joined honor and charm, truth and joy, sweetness and goodwill, affection and action. And all these take their beginning from Christ, advance through Christ, and are perfected in Christ. . . . And thus, friend cleaving to friend in the spirit of Christ, is made with Christ but one heart and one soul, and so mounting aloft through degrees of love to friendship with Christ, he is made one spirit with him in one kiss.[3]

Such a love is characterized by wanting to lay oneself open to the other person, to reveal the places—in plain trust—at which one is most vulnerable. I will tell you who I am and what in me is least to be loved. And I will tell you who you are and what in you seems utterly loveable.

Rarely, I think, and it is sad to say it, does this deep spiritual love spring up between blood relatives. And yet it is our very image of the love between sisters and brothers, mothers and daughters, fathers and sons. The fact, however, is that a hardened politics in blood relationships often blocks the spontaneity of the gift and makes the love seem owed, not freely given.

Perhaps Augustine and Monica are the exception:

Not long before the day on which she was to leave this life . . . we were talking alone together and our conversation was serene and joyful. . . .

Our conversation led us to the conclusion that no bodily pleasure, however great it might be . . . was worthy of comparison, or even of mention, beside the happiness of the life of the saints.

As the flame of love burned stronger in us and raised us higher towards the eternal God, our thoughts ranged over the whole compass of material things . . . up to the heavens themselves. . . .

Higher still we climbed. . . .

And while we spoke of the eternal Wisdom, longing for it and straining for it with all the strength of our hearts, for one fleeting instant we reached out and touched it.[4]

So binding are these spiritual ties that they transcend old kinships. So as we grow in Christ, we grow into new families, formed by a deep common love of God. The bond, it seems, is sacramental.

How often these deep friendships seem to spring up among those who experience the Eucharist together. Or among those who—if they are not present at one Eucharist—nevertheless know Christ in the Eucharist as the very life and center of their prayer.

It is as though his presence in the Eucharist were flung out like a huge net in which he catches us. As we tumble about, we find each other, sisters and brothers in our eucharistic love, and discover ourselves to be fish, not out of water but in the water where we belong.

But it is not only in the Eucharist that this happens. It is in every sharing of the word, broken like bread and distributed among us, feeding one or two intimately and fully as it feeds five thousand.

I hear a priest preaching, a priest whose name I don't know, whose face I don't recognize. But in his preaching I know the Lord himself, in the word this stranger lovingly brings to me. And without knowing him in any human way, I am suddenly caught up in an intense sense of friendship with him. We are one.

I meet a young man on the floor of an exhibit hall at a convention. He tells me that he is a Christian, and he shares some uncertainties of his life, his need to move from one city to another, his confusion about where to go, and I tell him that I, too, am Jonah, sent to Nineveh, not knowing why or for what reason the Lord has asked me to go.

And we are caught up, suddenly, in the intense burning that is were-not-our-hearts-burning-together-on-the-road, and we know Christ together, present with us, in each other. We are strangers turned intimates. Christ has bound us together with ties that are spiritual steel.

Slowly we begin to comprehend what the Lord is doing in this kind of love. How he is making one family out of us, a Church, built out of countless individualities, held together by affectionate, invisible bonds:

> You give us grace upon grace
> to build the temple of your spirit
> creating its beauty from the holiness of our lives.
> Your house of prayer
> is also the promise of the Church in heaven.
> Here your love is always at work,
> preparing the Church on earth for its heavenly glory. . . .[5]

Between Christians who pray there is a magnetic field: an attraction more powerful than any merely human passion, but like human passion. The passion of this friendship drives us to holiness. That is its distinguishing mark.

Between Christians of opposite sexes the sudden intensity of this friendship—the white heat—may be terrifying at first. It is an eros, so like the drive that makes us want to throw everything over, every commitment, every fidelity, in behalf of simple concentration on or dwelling in the other person.

But it is possible to see and know Christ glowing in the center of that fire, turning us to himself, shaping us to virtue, calling us to prayer, refining us to do his work. The love that strikes two in Christ is the same passion that makes three or more—any number—flame into holiness. It is passion that leads to God's service and to prayer.

Is the Enemy lurking somewhere in the wings, waiting for

someone to make a false move? Unquestionably, he sees these moments of passion as a definite opportunity. No sense laughing him off or forgetting his lingering presence in the neighborhood. At the same time, we can trust in Paul's word to us that neither principalities nor powers nor height nor depth nor any other creature can separate us from the love that is Christ Jesus our Lord.

Some of the great saints, most open to friendship, most chiseled and perfected by it, have felt this fear and ambivalence about it as well. But they also sensed that these affections were opportunities for holiness. Such passions are not mere temptations but turning points. The eros we experience can be lived out in faithfulness as a way to God. It is he who makes us burn for him, and for him in each other. And he has made those others to love us and be loved by us.

Friendship is part of the way of fidelity. It is not the pleasure-seeking of the person who merely wants friends as gratifications, the friendship-seeking that C. S. Lewis thought one of the saddest human traits of all. Friendships-in-God are not found by seeking friendship, but by seeking God. Those who draw closer to God find such friendships simply burst upon them. These bombshells of intense affection explode without warning in our lives. But they are good surprises.

> How good, how delightful it is
>   for all to live together like brothers:
>
> fine as oil on the head,
>   running down the beard,
> running down Aaron's beard
>   to the collar of his robes;
>
> copious as a Hermon dew
>   falling on the heights of Zion,
> where Yahweh confers his blessing,
>   everlasting life.[6]

Perhaps the most striking observation one could make about such friendships has to do with the way they become intensified after one of the partners dies. The friendship is strengthened and purified, it seems, by this death, which we say is not cessation but passage into deeper perception of God. The presence of that person becomes more so in the lives of those left behind. It is as though the blinding intensity of heaven were being shared, over the boundary, and the life of God were flowing more readily into us through them.

By this experience we become more confident of the communion of saints. They no longer seem to be, in the figure Ronald Knox used, figures looking down from heaven through a muslin floor. More than that, they are true partners with us in prayer and experience, and we know, by the passage of one friend into their company, that we, too, will someday be there.

This friendship is friendship with God and with others because of God. It is a friendship not of the flesh, but of adoption, a spiritual bond that echoes Shakespeare's words:

> Those friends thou hast, and their adoption tried,
> Grapple them to thy soul with hoops of steel. . . .[7]

But the grappling is done not by us, but by grace. In the steel that holds us together—the metal of faith and reverence—we know ourselves not only brothers and sisters, but joint-heirs in Christ. The steel is invisible, but tried in the fire and very safe to lean on.

NOTES

1. 1 Samuel 18:1.
2. 2 Timothy 1:3–4, 6–7.
3. Aelred of Rievaulx, *Spiritual Friendship*, trans. Mary Eugenia Laker (Kalamazoo, Mich.: Cistercian Publications, 1977), pp. 74–75.
4. Augustine, *Confessions*, trans. R. S. Pine-Coffin (London: Penguin Books, 1961) pp. 196–97.
5. Preface for Dedication of a Church II, Roman Sacramentary.
6. Psalm 133.
7. William Shakespeare, *Hamlet*, Act I, Scene iii, line 62.

6. Fear of Heights

For each of us the way lies straight ahead. There is, immediately in front of us, an appointed task, a call: some difficult, clear, utterly simple thing the Lord is asking us to do. It is not a general admonition to whoever might happen to be standing about. It is instead an utterly private request whispered, as it were, into each one's ear. What the Lord is asking me, he is asking no one else. More than likely, it is a request with no particular glamor or notoriety attached to it. And if I pay attention, the Lord leaves me in no doubt about it. Especially if I ask in prayer, he tells me very clearly. (Which is why, sometimes, I don't hurry to find out.)

And I cannot accomplish this thing God asks without grace. The call, this request is completely beyond my grasp, quite impossible—without his help. Yet even as he asks it, he makes it clear that his grace will be poured out. He will give me the power to do what is needed. He will not leave me abandoned or alone. He does not ask the impossible. Our God does not play tricks. Or, to put it another way, when he asks the impossible, we remember that nothing is impossible with God.

But why are we surprised by this? We knew from the beginning that prayer would bring us closer to the mind of God, more able to know his thoughts and do his will. We knew that, yet when by a kind of radar we sense it, when we feel ourselves being moved and led in a given direction, we feel awe, we are afraid. Afraid perhaps that we are acting, actors in a drama we did not design. Somehow a story has been set in motion and the characters are mainly two: God and I. It is a dance! It is a suspense story. It is leading to an unknown destination. It is once-upon-a-time, and now, and what-is-yet-to-be, all at once. It is now and forever, and yet it is not a dream. It is happening and it is real.

And now there is no turning back. The commitment has already been made: the escalator is ascending, the elevator door is closing, the plane is moving along the runway. Something very definite has been set in motion, is gathering momentum, is picking up speed. It seems we can hardly stop now, especially when the journey is starting to get interesting! Even so, we are fearful. Now that the cabin door is closed and the motors are revving, the shudder and the trembling are perhaps not so exhilarating as we had thought.

Yet, we have signed on for this. We are here by our own consent. Even if there should be pain interwoven with this commitment, some intimation of suffering to come, there is, at the same time, a knowing—we know Who it is that's asking and this intimate sense of a God who loves us is present even when he is leading us into the furnace or the deep. Our God will not betray us. He is just and fair and tender. He does not forget us in the time of trouble, he that keeps Israel does not slumber or sleep.

So we go on, straight ahead, with no more sense of direction than just to make the next step and the next. We are not out to make high jumps, to take three steps at a time. There is no longer much question of spiritual ambition or advancing in prayer. We have no sense of height. We can't tell whether or not we are ascending. If we are climbing (and we are), we sense that only in our muscles and bones. The climb is costly. But it does not feel upward. It is not a high. It is neither consolation nor desolation.

It is ascent, but not ecstasy. In a sense, it is deeper than ecstasy, or perhaps one could call it the ecstasy of every day, a union that continues while everything else is also happening, existing within whatever activities are necessary, an abandonment known only to us and God, ecstatic only in that it is so very complete.

This abandonment is the very heart and essence of Christian prayer, and it has nothing in common with strategy and second-guessing. It is the pray-to-win mentality turned inside out, and yet it is not a pray-to-lose mentality. It is the prayer that has moved beyond intending, directing, steering, second-guessing God. It is the dancer moving completely in the rhythm of the partner, prayer that is utterly freeing because it is completely at one. Utterly beyond asking, beyond the anger that rattles heaven's gate. Prayer that does not plead, wants nothing for itself but what God wants, it is the will-not-to-will, rooted in grace, that makes it possible to be abandoned, free, and then (by some further miracle) able to act with a semblance of coherence and freedom even when completely surrendered to and possessed by the loving will of God.

And it is this abandonment that is meant when we are told to drop our nets and follow him; to pause not to bury our dead fathers or tell our wives we will be traveling for a while; it is in this abandonment that we sell all.

That is not to say that we no longer can experience loss and mourn what we lose. More and more, with greater intensity, we love the things we are losing and we drink in the temporary beauty of life with a real thirst. Every experience of genuine pleasure is fully tasted, not with the connoisseur's boredom born of sampling a dozen wines to know what's best, but instead with the delight that makes this glass the most enjoyable. When flowers bloom, we bury our noses in them and look up again like Disney creatures, covered with pollen and surrounded by bees. Like Bambi on the ice, we still hurl ourselves into possibility and find, to our surprise, that we are "kinda wobbly." But increasingly, as we climb the steps of prayer, it becomes less possible to covet pleasure and flee from pain. Each experience—pleasant or painful—becomes a call. The empty hour, the agonizing instant, the intolerable stretch of pain, the whine of the dentist's drill, the click of the X-ray machine, the helplessness of being wheeled into surgery, the cry of the anguished person we would help if we could, but can't reach out to—all this consciousness of the negative calls us to the heights. We climb with tears and a deepening dependence on the God we cannot see or hear. Through prayer, expectation is reversed. Reality seems otherwise than it did. The amusements and pastimes that once seemed the only sure flight from pain are now the very things we flee from. Every step up the mountain road, every bramble across the face, every ankle twisted on a stone, every stumbling in the underbrush—

these adversities harden us, shape us to our purpose, and at the same time open us to possibilities of suffering and grief.

The pain and the pleasure are two faces of the same coin: experience itself. And they are an unmistakable gift from God. This consciousness begins to make a little sense out of our existence, which otherwise would have no shape at all. That gift, now, slowly, by small degrees, carrying us upward, makes it possible now and then to gaze into the eyes of death—bemused, curious, wondering—wanting somehow to circle past the mask to the face of Christ waiting on the other side.

To be called to the heights in prayer, however briefly, is to sense a new relationship with God beginning, and to be afraid.

It is a definite summons within the summons of prayer itself. It is conversion-beyond-conversion. And when the summons comes, there is a real suspicion, all at once, that the ticket may be for a one-way ride.

Death is now the destination. While no particular number has been revealed, a number has nevertheless been assigned. We don't know the day or the hour. But there is momentum now, there is urgency. Life has a real term and time has to be dealt with.

Winter is no longer winter, a time of year to be gotten through with scarves and snow plows and mittens. It is winter carved more deeply into us because of all the winters that have gone before. Winter is more wintry—its special character etched by repetition, the noise of banging shutters sharpened by familiarity—we have heard it all so many times before. Yet *this* winter has in it a certain number of nights and says and slips past with a velocity that reminds us we are ruled by time. Because we are older, we know winter: winter itself, shaped like no other thing.

And with time, the list of these uniquely shaped things grows. The intense, collective joy of a public celebration—the visit of a king, a pope—or the heightened sorrow of some disaster—a planecrash in a suburb, killing all, fifteen minutes of death that reverberates for weeks and months in the consciousness of all who know about it. A murder, a kidnapping, an assassination, a strike, a power failure, a christening, a wedding—each sort of event is heightened in its uniqueness by a sense that such events are "unto themselves," not quite like anything.

When we lived in New York, I remember that a certain day in June was celebrated on Flagpole Green in Forest Hills as Children's Day. It could hardly be called a tradition, yet it seemed to happen each year in more or less the same way. There were adult volunteers in straw hats selling cokes, hot dogs, and beer. A tall, silver-haired man in a top hat announced races and competitions for children by megaphone. Rides-on-trucks parked at the curbstones, with children and anxious-looking mothers lined up waiting. An overamplified band made whiny, semi-electronic sounds somewhere on the periphery. Most important of all, there were children: all ages and shapes, running, tussling, giggling, getting lost. The children were different each year. Some had moved in. Others had moved away. Yet the event seemed to have a cumulative reality, becoming more itself each year. It somehow gained a character, an imprint in the memory, so that if someone were to say, "There won't be any Children's Day in Forest Hills next year," this news would be followed by a sigh. Something entirely *itself* would cease to be.

And if this is the case with a mere "made-up" event, how much more so with hallowed events and times. The word *Christmas* conveys to each of us a very particular set of sensations and feelings. But not only Christmas. Events themselves have a character, heightened by repetition. There is a web of feeling and memory interconnecting things: "Do you remember Pearl Harbor? The day John F. Kennedy died? Do you remember radio?" It is not a solitary but a collective memory of some keenly felt experience. The sharpening effect of time and reflection and recognition and recollection—all these together produce a heightening that is, by an odd, unanticipated twist, a hint of bliss.

Everything changes. The kaleidoscope picture of our experience is constantly shattered, dispersed, tiny beads of shape and color rearranging themselves into the next design. At moments in the company of another, and more than one, events make sense, have a pattern, somewhere. Then the image breaks once again. Yet we are conscious somehow that the "it" which cannot be grasped or held contant is experience itself. And that experience, however painful, is God's sharing of his reality, a gift from his hand.

Now our understanding of Providence must change. Once we had thought Providence was what kept bad things from happening. A thousand would fall, and ten thousand, and not come nigh me. Now it is clear that we, too, are falling, dying, losing our grip, entering into the death-that-is-not, reminding ourselves as we fall, "If a man keep my saying, he shall never see death."

Well, does it exist? Is it real or isn't it?

Doesn't it seem that death must be tasted in order for us to say that it is not, and then, perhaps, we will already not be?

Or have we been clutching at straws, following whoever would promise a reprieve from death?

But then, didn't our Savior die? And wasn't it his dying that gave us the model of how to die?

Therefore, isn't death the parachute jump already made once-for-all in which the chute, most definitely and without question, *did* open?

And since he has already died our death for us, isn't it true that death no longer is and that we will not die?

But isn't it also true that each of us who has been baptized into the Lord Jesus has been baptized into his death?

And isn't his death—our chance to share it—the hope we are living for?

Death as conclusion, resolution, transcendence, insight, breakthrough, revelation, transformation?

Doesn't it become more and more plain as we approach it, that death is as real as, perhaps more real than, another experience? Isn't it our fear that makes us want to say it is not real?

Death is that something—the evidence of which we can see—that we say is not because we do not want it to be. Something we say is not, because our Savior transcended it, strangled it, redefined it, overcame it. Does his rising mean death is not real? Or does it mean that death is real but temporary?

Isn't it, after all, an optical illusion? A passage through some invisible sort of wall over which or through which we immortals can then look back at our struggling fellows, observe, encourage, and pray for them?

All our efforts to imagine death and the afterlife stumble and limp. Messages from the beyond do not convince. Those who are in touch with their departed dear ones sound hopeful, but as though their messages were entrusted to them alone. We have Moses and the prophets and the word of the Lord that these should be enough for us. Even if one were to rise from the dead, many would not be convinced. The issue is not one of proofs and plausibility, but of faith and trust. Emily Dickinson puts it well when she says death is a riddle through which, at the last, sagacity must go.

Whatever death is, it is a corollary of time. And if in prayer it cannot be said that we come to love and anticipate death (though there are moments when that seems to be so, I think we don't ever really *love* death), what can be said is that, in prayer and by prayer, we become reconciled to time.

"I don't want to die," my child said to me, "except so I can go to heaven." She summed it up well, I thought. The joy of heaven was a vivid possibility worth dying for. Somehow her statement made it seem that we might hop, skip, and jump our way there.

But there is more to getting to heaven than that. There is the need for dying all along. There is the need to accept, entirely and without question, the odd quirk of vision that comes about with the passing of time, the rubbing and burnishing that comes from the sheer flow of events over us. There is the need to stifle within ourselves those last-ditch instincts to run the other way, to reinvent youth and madcap impulses, as though they were worth having, as though (delusionary thought) youth were an exemption from time, as though reality could somehow be eluded by renting a car, taking a long trip, splurging, having a love-affair— cheating time by a sudden scramble up and over the wall. As though, when we scrambled down the other side, the shortness of our lives, the reality of our situation, the hurtling fact of our destiny moving towards closure, would not be simply waiting to confront us on the other side.

Vita brevis! Our limitations must be looked squarely in the eye. And yet it is not all so very simple and clear as that. Ten years is a wink. Twenty years are day before yesterday. Events long buried in childhood swim into consciousness with a new immediacy even as they recede in time. Our dreams are peopled with those we haven't seen for decades. Now we see that time is a clown and a trickster. It is an odd predicament in which we find ourselves. Like Cyrano, we want to take up arms against our old enemy and find him constantly eluding the *epee*.

Yet by our constant reaching for God, we are climbing. And because our ascent is steep, we must prepare for the unexpected: our altitude may change suddenly in flight. In which case, the oxygen mask in front of us will drop automatically . . . or it will not drop and existence itself will drop away, experience will plummet, consciousness will swoop, a sudden curvature will twist our destiny into a nose dive.

What then if there had been no aviation? What if we had kept our feet planted on the ground? What if we had never gone coasting at 37,000 feet, across acres of lambswool clouds, the cabin flooded with sunshine? What if we had been plain cowards, running from confrontations, never knowing the heady release of placing our lives in the hands of God? What if we had lived all along as though we were the masters of the universe?

What if there had been no trust? No abandonment to his will, no assent to good and not-so-good, no being pushed and pulled by Providence? What if Christ had fled from Gethsemane, saying, "Not your will but mine"?

What a cramped, boxed-in definition of reality that would be. It is clear now as we grow in Christ that the way out of this narrowing space—out of this burning building where the flames are ascending floor by floor—is up and out of the window, onto a narrow ledge where we can do nothing but crawl, one step after another, till we are safe and free. The way through into

freedom is by way of the potion Juliet drank, the one that coun-
terfeits death, the one we trust will allow us to wake up later on.

But what if it does not? What if God is a poor apothecary and
gets the prescriptions mixed? Or what if there is no apothecary
fixing the potions? What if the messenger from Verona loses his
way on the road, and there is no rhyme or reason, no real plot-
line after all?

As our faith advances, so does the sophistication of our doubt.
Some mechanism within the psyche constantly entertains the op-
posing viewpoint and, in the pitch of the battle, sits down with
the enemy general for tea. How would I live if there were no
God? What would I rip off? Whom would I betray? How would I
indulge myself? What riches would I lay up? And the longer one
entertains the "other side," the more the answer grows: If there
were no God at all, still I would believe in him! If he had not sent
his son to me, all the same I would take up my cross. The intensified life we have tasted in prayer makes us believe in heaven by
conviction alone, even when reason shouts us down:

> This world is not conclusion;
>   A sequel stands beyond,
> Invisible, as music,
>   But positive as sound.[1]

It is not the ecstasy of the great mystics, frozen, timeless, days-
on-end, can't-feel-a-pinprick ecstasy—but rather our own taste
of God's love that convinces us. Now we know heaven is real
because we are allowed to visit there once in awhile.

> My soul rejoices in my God,
> for he has clothed me in the garments of salvation,
> he has wrapped me in the cloak of integrity,
> like a bridegroom . . .
> like a bride. . . .[2]

Let us not suppose ecstasy is ruled out for ordinary people like
ourselves. It is not as though we had invented it, or as though we
had written the rules. The Lord seizes us suddenly with a quick

burst of affection. His power flows to us. He sweeps us up. Everything else stands still for a kiss that is passionate, tender, demanding. In anticipation of this kiss, whole lives are altered and overturned. In the aftermath of this kiss, destinies and ambitions and careers are discarded like old pairs of gloves. This is the sign of a love in which there is no disenchantment, no chance of boredom, no ultimate letdown. All is climax. This kiss is the pledge of a union that feeds and heals us, clothes and shelters us, that makes us Christ.

But who is this Lover of mine? Is he the Father, whom I approach through his Son? Is he the Son whom I ask to bring me closer to his Father? Do I open myself to the breath of the Spirit blowing through me, carrying me before him as by a storm of grace? Who is this Person into whose arms I run?

Before me there is a whirlwind, and in the center of the whirlwind is a still, small voice, saying, I am.

I am, before the world was made.

I am, that to which all the world is striving, the love to which all eros drives, the food for which all hunger reaches.

I am, the shepherd on the hillside, bearing you up in my arms.

Loving Ephraim when he was a child.

Giving my angels charge over you, to keep you in all your ways. Letting them bear you up, lest you dash your foot. Letting you tread on the lion, the adder, the young lion, and the dragon.

Telling you to untie your sandals, for the place where you're standing is holy ground.

Leading you beside the still waters.

Tipping the pitcher and dousing your head with holy oil.

Better one day in my courts, than a thousand in the tents of wickedness.

At the heights, this is how he speaks, not only to Moses and the prophets, but to us. He asks us to cut loose, to be his, to be unbound, attached to nothing but heaven and him. He asks us to unravel everything that binds us, everything that holds us in the here and now, to come as we are, now, without a change of clothing, without looking back, on a way from which there is no turning back: a strange and unconsoling path along a hidden and unglamorous way.

And so, by prayer, we gain the heights. We are not yet at the summit, nowhere near. The valley we have come from is long ago lost in fog, and the path has turned so often that there is no chance of turning back. We cannot see a foot ahead or behind. And the figure on the path ahead, just glimpsed now and then, seems to be carrying a cross. Our feet hurt just a little. The brambles seem to come from nowhere, and they scratch, most unpredictably. But for some odd reason we are smiling. We are not just roaming, poking around, exploring. Not at all. This course we are on is worth pursuing. Because it has a meaning. Because God has set the course for us. However little we can see the purpose, we know we are on the way.

Oh, my God, let me not be afraid, no matter how high I am, knowing that you are near and that are the maker and originator and master of the heights.

Therefore we shall not fear, though the mountains be removed and thrown into the sea, and though the waters roar. For the God in whom we trust, the keeper of Israel, does not slumber nor sleep. He is mindful of his promises. Most of all, he does not betray.

NOTES

1. Emily Dickinson, *Selected Poems and Letters of Emily Dickinson*, ed. Robert N. Linscott (New York: Doubleday and Company, 1959), p. 135.
2. Isaiah 61:10.

7. Clinging

Lovers make outrageous promises, forever promises, promises they can't keep. In all sincerity, they swear a love that won't die, that will grow in intensity, that will remain at the heights for a lifetime. And when they promise it, they believe it. It is the constant theme of love songs old and new:

> If ever I cease to love
> If ever I cease to love
> May the moon be turned into green cheese
> May fish grow legs and cows lay eggs
> If ever I cease to love.[1]

Yet even the most faithful lovers on earth can never sustain the heights of passion they felt at first blush. No matter how constant their love becomes—enduring, growing, going somewhat underground to become a mature and manageable affection—always, even the most generous love must fall short. The falling short is because we are human. Our humanity constantly aspires to more than it can do. Even saints are not perfectly loving. They quarrel with God and with each other. The most virtuous life is constricted by its humanity. As Browning told us, our reach exceeds our grasp.

But the Lord's love is unceasing. It is the one sort of love we can experience here and now that doesn't blow hot and cold. However much he courts us like a lover, chasing us down with an exquisite tenderness, nevertheless he doesn't play games with us as human lovers do. He doesn't tease us. He doesn't try to throw us off balance, just for his own amusement. The Greek deities, we have heard, used to send trials to mortals merely for their sport. From their Olympian peak, they looked down on human struggles like contests at the public games. But our God, the God of Israel, doesn't play games of that sort. His love for us is constant, unswerving. His forgiveness is all-at-once and without reserve. His love is both instantaneous and everlasting.

Yet we experience trials. We say they are tests, and so they are. Not that God is playing games with us. Far from it. Instead, as our love deepens and our capacities grow, he lets us share in the very reality that lies at the center of things. And we sense this growth as a cross. The stretching is painful. But in the letter of James, we are told not to think, ever, that evils are sent to us from God. Yet God lets us stand toe to toe and face to face with the evil that there is. He lets us be confronted by it, fight with it, flee from it, feel the pain of it. Somehow, in ways we don't understand, God is attacking those same evils in a different way, twisting and bending them till they mean good for us. The evils that whistle past our ears are the sign that we are saved. And without any clear vision or understanding of the matter, we must hold on and trust. Let go of our fear and frailty. We must depend on God. We must rely on him, embrace him. We must cling.

We must cling to the one reality that does not crumple. The one rock that will not be washed loose in the tide and onslaught of anything. We must cling to the one reality that will hold firm, though the earth be destroyed and the mountains flung into the sea and the sun put out. We must cling to the One who holds eternity in his hand, who will not perish in the end, and who has power to save us, too. The One who knew us before we existed, in whose thought and by whose hand we exist from moment to moment. He chose and shaped us from our mother's womb to be intimate with him. This intimacy is what we were made for. Away from it, we feel at odds with existence and even with ourselves. Close to him, we are at peace. This is the one intimacy of which we need not be afraid, for it will not disappoint or betray us. On God we can loose all the intensity of what we are, all the passion and the longing we feel. This is the one surrender we can make in utter trust, knowing that we can rest our whole weight there and nothing will give way.

This clinging will no doubt make us foolish in the eyes of the world. Even among our fellow Christians, it can make us a little conspicuous. When we speak of it, we are likely to hear talk of neurosis and escape from reality. But the escape into God is a break for freedom. We are, and must be, defectors from attachments and entanglements. We must flee into him, hide in him, just to have our strength renewed and to find the energy to serve him here and now:

> ... Those who hope in Yahweh renew their strength,
> they put out wings like eagles.
> They run and do not grow weary,
> walk and never tire.[2]

And the more we cling, the more we experience strength not as what we do, but what God does in us. The more we understand that when we ask, he will give us the words to say. Like Stephen, we ask for the Spirit of God to give us the words we lack—and when the time comes, we have the courage and the words. When the high hillsides loom before us, we are afraid. But by clinging and knowing that God is our strength, we find, one step at a time, that we are ascending, not by any doing of our own, but purely by his grace.

By this clinging, then, we become aware of a closeness that can hardly be spoken of—something deeper than words that can't be really conveyed in speech of any kind; something that joins us to God, that hallows us in an unaccountable way; something that alters and changes us in a way that seems chemical. For it is making of us what we were not and never dared hope to be:

> ... I found him whom my heart loves.
> I held him fast, nor would I let him go. . . .[3]

This fusion, this fastening onto God, this barnacle dependency is the very clinging of which I set out to tell: the bonding that makes us one with God. Yet we are more than the barnacles are. For ours is not a helpless tagging onto a powerful Other, but instead an embrace that is completely and unreservedly mutual. He has made us for himself and we find our rest in him.

> In God alone there is rest for my soul,
>   from him comes my safety;
> with him alone for my rock, my safety,
>   my fortress, I can never fall.[4]

When we say that prayer is clinging, we imagine ourselves holding on by a thread over an abyss of devastation. And it is true that God is our reality, our deliverance, the power that rescues us from nonbeing by the mere fact of conceiving us and holding us in his thought. He loved us into existence first; he holds us in existence now. The Lord has numbered every hair of our heads. The limit of our days is known to him. God is greater than we, greater than our hearts. It is this we remember when we call prayer a clinging. Not only that we cling to God, but that he clings to us.

> Because you are precious in my eyes,
> Because you are honored and I love you,
> I give men in exchange for you,
> peoples in return for your life.
> Do not be afraid, for I am with you.[5]

The love is a mutual love. It is a mutual embrace. We are not flirting with God, dancing attention on him, winning his favor, trying to gain him somehow. He is the One who loved us first. He began this relationship. He poured his passion out on us. The love we feel is a response to his love. We sense that we are not entirely the authors of our prayer. Rather, as Evelyn Underhill tells us,

Prayer means . . . taking our part, however humble, tentative and half-understood, in the continual conversation, the communion, of our spirits with the Eternal Spirit; the acknowledgment of our entire dependence, which is yet the partly free dependence of the child. For Prayer is really our whole life toward God: our longing for Him, our incurable "God-sickness," as Barth calls it, our whole drive towards Him.[6]

When we cling, then, we are responding, returning the embrace in which he holds us. His love is constant, powerful, enthusiastic. Our love fluctuates, ebbs and flows. There are times when we don't feel like loving and don't want to be loved. We go stiff in his embrace. We want to remain in a certain standoffish coldness where we can be empty, lonely, sorry for ourselves. Then prayer is the conscious and determined act by which we shatter our own self-imposed isolation and move, slowly at first, then ever more passionately, into a responsive embrace: a clinging to God which is a commitment, a compact, a covenant, an act of utter trust: that union with God which is beyond speech, beyond reason, beyond thought—a real surrender to the burning intensity of God's love.

> He has taken me to his banquet hall
> and the banner he raises over me is love. . . .
> His left arm is under my head,
> his right embraces me.[7]

The keen pleasure and intimacy of this closeness to God is described by George Herbert as a love-meeting. It is one in which the self feels inadequate to the encounter, but God makes everything right.

> Love bade me welcome: yet my soul drew back,
>   Guilty of dust and sin.
> But quick-eyed Love, observing me grow slack
>   From my first entrance in,
> Drew nearer to me, sweetly questioning,
>   If I lacked anything.
>
> A guest, I answered, worthy to be here:
>   Love said, You shall be he.
> I, the unkind, ungrateful? Ah my dear,
>   I cannot look on thee.
> Love took my hand, and smiling, did reply,
>   "Who made the eyes but I?"
>
> Truth Lord, but I have marred them: let my shame
>   Go where it doth deserve.
> And know you not, says Love, who bore the blame?
>   My dear, then I will serve.
> You must sit down, says Love, and taste my meat.
>   So I did sit and eat.[8]

In this intimacy, in this full dependency and closeness there is freedom, the only freedom we are likely to taste here and now. It is a freedom that comes about not from doing, but from undoing: letting go of all the support systems that sustained us, or seemed to sustain us, before now. It is a clinging that sharpens our detachment. To depend on God, we must stop depending on anyone or anything human. Yet this very detachment is what frees us to hold our friends to our hearts most tenderly, without domination of them or by them, without unreasonable expectations of what friendship and human love can accomplish or provide.

We find it painful to let go of our friends, and yet the keenest pain on earth can come from holding on too hard. We live on their admiration. We feel powerful when they praise us. Sometimes we can't move a step without their reassurance. We lack confidence in our own opinions. We need them to say we are lovable and good. Sometimes we find one or two others who will consistently affirm us. We are happy for a time, until something we do, surprisingly, displeases them. Suddenly we are shattered. Because we have been clinging to friends for support, we have left ourselves open for defeat and dismay. The detached love of Christian friends is other than that. I love you, I say, but I do not need you to tell me who I am. For the Lord himself does that, when he whispers his love in my ear every day. Every day he creates me anew and sharpens my identity by grace. From him comes strength. He gives me my confidence, my self-assurance. He awakens my sense of destiny. Because of him, I know that the future stretches ahead, and he is calling me to find it. And when I walk together with him, even when I can't see my hand in front of me, I am sure. And you, my friend, may walk together with us—with my Lord and with me. And we will share our love generously with you. But I will not lean on any human being for God-support. When God sends his grace through another person, I will remember God first for that. I will praise God first for that. I will cherish the friend who was my channel of grace. But I will not, dare not, make a god of her or him. I will not lean too hard on my friends. I know their frailties as I know my own.

Most of all, I will not be beguiled, entirely, by the ones who promise to be wiser than I and pretend to have no weaknesses! I will not trust my future fully to any authority figures. Now that I am grown, I will not be Galatea to anyone's Pygmalion. It is the Lord, the Lord only, who will chisel me out and shape me to the destiny he has in mind. I will stand free and clear of entanglements, not clinging to anyone human, not calling any man father, and serving only the God who made heaven and earth and chose Israel for his own.

So, with this will-to-be-free-in-God, I say I am completely his—moving and breathing and having my being in him alone. Open to the breath of the spirit. Wanting to live completely by his command. Caring not for tomorrow, especially not concerned to second-guess the future by laying up treasures on earth. Making investments in prayer-installments, paid daily, without calculating the interest or counting the cost. My reward, when it comes, to stand in the place he has made for me and look on his face.

Clinging! That is the ecstasy the saints have told about. What they didn't always tell us was that it was so close by, as simple as turning one's face to the Lord instead of to the wall. What they did not fully describe to us was how suddenly the spirit of God can be present, whenever, by an act of the will, we put ourselves into his company. It can happen in a moment, any moment. And when we have time for it, and the moments stretch out into an ocean of time, there is the chance, always, that our clinging will carry us along so far it feels as if there will be no returning.

For when we are with him, conventional time ceases to be and the ordinary ways of measuring our existence slip away. There is no clock, no calendar, no rotation of the earth. Instead we enter a place beyond place, a region that is always now. A zone to be found only with the heart, a country where one does not either see or hear. It is a place of stillness and peace, but one where the flame of love so burns in us that it seems likely to consume us. We ourselves are the burning bush that is somehow not consumed.

As the Father has loved me,
so I have loved you.
Remain in my love.[9]

And in this mystery of the presence of God, we understand nothing and we grasp everything. We swing by a gossamer thread in a space that is not space and a country that exists nowhere but in the heart.

For myself, I prefer to be lost in this nowhere, wrestling with this blind nothingness. . . . Don't worry if your faculties fail to grasp it. Actually, that is the way it should be, for this nothingness is so lofty that they cannot reach it. . . .[10]

And we hold on, with a knowing that is closer and more intimate than thought, at a point that is both infinity and zero, spinning out to the very corner of existence where the immeasurable sense of God compels and seizes us and cradles us in a knowing that is all and the promise of more than all.

I call you friends,
because I have made known to you
everything that I learned from my Father.[11]

Peace! Peace that is ecstasy and release, climax and consummation, contradiction and resolution, and with all that, a kind of crazy joy that builds in us until we want to shout: Our God is real! He is there, just there, cherishing you, desiring me, coaxing and beguiling us, until we are simply drunk with his closeness and his love.

Delirious and yet calm and content, made happy by the simple knowledge of God and the place he has prepared for us.

You did not choose me,
no, I chose you;
and I commissioned you
to go out and to bear fruit,
fruit that will last;
and then the Father will give you
anything you ask in my name.[12]

Who on earth could ever be this for me? And now that I have tasted him, now that he has made himself known to me, how could I look in the courts of sinners for any other lover, how could I be false to the vision I have seen?

For it is better to live one day with such a Lord than a thousand with any other lover.

There is no money on earth to buy such treasure, and yet the Lord has scattered it to the winds, blowing like tufts of dandelion, free to be gathered up by anyone who will take the time to pray.

By those who will dare to risk the possibility that God is real. To gamble their whole lives on heaven and the high stakes of the kingdom.

To scatter their earthly possessions, to sell all they have of material reassurance and be conscious that there is no insurance anywhere unless it is under the shadow of his wing.

To those who will dare everything, cutting loose from second-guessing and false security, to those who will walk the stony, narrow path, to those he will give the riches of the kingdom, the vision that is to come:

> My son, if you desire to serve the Lord,
>   prepare yourself for an ordeal. . . .
> Cling to him and do not leave him,
>   so that you may be honored at the end of your days.[13]

Or perhaps you will not be honored, as the world measures honor. But in that inward chamber of the heart, he will honor you there. There he will pour the oil of wisdom over your head and will lay out fine garments for you. He will anoint you as a son and heir and will gather you close to him.

Not only afterwards, when all the books are opened and read. But here and now, when you withdraw from the rush and clamor of your existence, even now he will cover you with riches when you cling to him.

And that secret smile you carry with you, that startled look when people surprise you and you were praying just then, that look of the clinging-prayer, working within you and transforming you, that look betrays you. It gives you away.

Your heart is brimming over with love, and the love is not the barren love of one who reaches beyond himself and is scorned and mistreated and shoved aside.

The love that is beyond all loves is your Master and your Lord, and when you cling to him, he remembers you, he cherishes you, he sets you on high, he floods you with strength and holiness and light.

This is the clinging that grows more so with every chance at prayer, with every Eucharist, every acknowledgment of sin, every repentance, every conversion of heart.

This is the clinging that changes us, moment by moment, into the image God had in mind when he first thought of us. Until that moment when we can be face to face with him.

Like Dorothy, we have always had the power to go back to Kansas—to journey from Oz to Kansas and back again by a simple exertion of the will. The secret is in the wanting to. And the secret is so well kept, not because it is not easily guessed, but because so many of us are afraid to enter the Emerald City and confront the wizard who lives there.

So each one of us must make the discovery on her or his own (a discovery long hidden in a closet with old playthings and lost saints) that God has invented the universe to delight us. That his love is so much for each one alone that it seems as if the moon and stars had been made for our nursery windows and no other creature had occupied God's mind since time began. This childlike sense of being at the center of his thought and the apple of his eye is recovered by adults in prayer. At last we know the fairy tales are true and immortality is not a fake. The land will not be Oz, where witches are sometimes wicked and sometimes good, but a land where God is to be with us. And that knowing will be bliss.

By clinging, then, we come to know that heaven is not only later on, but has somehow already begun, and that the kingdom is at work in us with a silent greening, shooting up like spring while there is snow still on the ground.

By clinging to God, we sense the bonds that bind us to each other, heavenly and holy bonds we don't fully understand, bonds that, by the usual reversal of Christian experience, are not bonds of bondage but bonds that set us free.

For we are free together in Christ. Free enough to love not one at a time, but many at a time, and becoming every day more free of the petty rages and jealousies most earthly loves are heir to. In our prayer we begin to know the love we will live in the resurrection, when our knowing will be like that of the angels and our friendships will be mystical and free. When our love will be beyond measure, for we will see him as he is and will know even as we are known.

And everyone who has this hope in Him cleanses and purifies himself with faithfulness and fasting and the steadfast clinging that is prayer.

And we sense now that we are praying together. However much my love-meeting is God-and-I, it is also God-and-you-and-I. For the more God's love flows into me, the more that love crests and builds to a torrent in me that flows over into you. And that same powerful love runs among us and we are held together in a current of joy.

And this is true, however privately I go away to pray. For even when I approach the Lord in prayer just by myself, alone, from the corner of my eye I can sense those others praying with me. My brothers and sisters not only of this time, but of all time, are there in my prayer.

And there are some I know by name. I name them in my prayer. And there are some who, praying with me, bound together with me in my heart in prayer, are of one voice with me, and we pray to the Lord together. So it is that my most private prayer is the prayer of the Church somehow in a way I know to be true, but cannot either prove or understand:

Now with angels and archangels and the whole company of heaven we sing the unending hymn of your praise.[14]

To experience this is to experience heaven and at the same time to sharpen the ache that is a constant of our existence here and now. In prayer, for a time, all wounds are healed, all secrets whispered and made known, all hopes freshly kindled again, and a peace that is not so much tranquillity as intensity seizes our hearts and makes them whole.

And we experience, in a kind of alternation, the intimacy and closeness of being-with-God and the longing of being-without-God. The nearer we come to him, the closer he comes to us, the more we know we are not yet there—and yet, somehow, we are on the way.

This very unrealization seems to us the pledge and the promise of what is to come:

> Heaven is what I cannot reach!
>   The apple on the tree,
> Provided it do hopeless hang,
>   That "heaven" is, to me.[15]

Emily Dickinson, as usual, expresses it concisely. It is as though the constant reaching, the stretching, the intolerable yearning, the asking were in itself a token of the destination.

For when all is said and done, there is only this to say: no matter how sweet the event, how consoling the moment, there is always a deep longing within us that cuts like a knife. It is a yearning that stirs even when (or perhaps most often when) the air is flooded with sunshine and the sky dazzles us with color and light. Then this unutterable loneliness that we feel is in no way justified. Yet in the midst of our gratitude for the beauty of created things, we know in our very bones that there is something yet to be given. The emptiness is the mark and reminder of God. By this sense of what is not, we know what is and what is yet to be.

And the days flow and the seasons turn, and we hold on fast and for dear life we cling. Time slips through our fingers, and we know more and more how helpless we are, how utterly without recourse. And we surrender. We are reconciled. As we accept, more and more, what is, we are held tighter and tighter in the intimate knowledge that we are loved forever and a day, held close and cherished, rescued, forgiven, and redeemed.

And in our prayer, we are Jacob, for the angels are climbing not only up to God, but down to us. We are climbing Jacob's ladder and the energy is both ascending and descending, striking life into our hearts and killing us with the promise of bliss.

NOTES

1. "If Ever I Cease to Love," song from the burlesque musical, *Blue Beard,* adopted in 1872 as the official song of Mardi Gras in New Orleans.
2. Isaiah 40:31.
3. Song of Songs 3:4.
4. Psalm 62:1-2.
5. Isaiah 43:4-5.
6. Evelyn Underhill, *The Spiritual Life* (New York: Harper & Row, n.d.), p. 61.
7. Song of Songs 2:4, 6.
8. George Herbert, "Love (III)," *The Works of George Herbert,* ed. F. E. Hutchinson (Oxford: Clarendon Press, 1945), pp. 188–89 (spelling and punctuation modernized).
9. John 15:9.
10. William Johnston trans., *The Cloud of Unknowing* (New York: Doubleday Image, 1973), p. 136.
11. John 15:15.
12. John 15:16.
13. Ecclesiasticus 2:1, 3.
14. From the Roman Catholic liturgy of the Mass.
15. Emily Dickinson, *Selected Poems and Letters of Emily Dickinson,* ed. Robert N. Linscott (New York: Doubleday and Company, 1959), p. 78.

Afterword

Books are sometimes a better help than friends in a commitment to take prayer seriously. In fact, books are friends and supporters in that effort, spiritual partners of a sort. In that spirit of friendship, I would commend to the reader a few books that I found helpful in my initial commitment to prayer.

But, first, I would express a caution. This brief list is entirely my own and in no way represents a bibliography, even a partial bibliography, of prayer. The Christian literature of prayer is vast and the contemporary literature is constantly growing. Any visit to a Christian bookstore will confirm that shelf after shelf of books on prayer and spirituality are readily available.

But my books, like my prayer life, represent a very personal choice: a choice to design for myself a way of coming closer to God that works for me in the context of my real experience and the demands of my own life.

I began with the monks, who rightly deserve, I think, to be our teachers and models in prayer. In particular, I cherish a battered copy of Andre Louf's *Teach Us to Pray: Learning a Little About God* (New York: Paulist Press, 1975). This small book by a French contemplative, who became the Abbot of the Trappist Monastery of Katsberg in 1963, is remarkably successful in describing the experience of prayer and inspiring others to it. For a lay person, perhaps, it is necessary, when reading Louf's book, to translate it into the context of her or his own life. But prayer is prayer, everywhere and for everyone. Louf is good at conveying the fact that prayer is a matter of inwardness. "This state of prayer," he writes, "is something we always carry about, like a hidden treasure of which we are not consciously aware—or hardly so." But Louf says it is possible for all of us to awaken to prayer and find that treasure within: "So it is not really hard to pray. It was given us long since. . . . Little by little it will saturate and captivate our faculties, mind and soul and body."[1] Two books by Thomas Merton can provide a similar starting point and refreshment in prayer: *Contemplative Prayer* (New York: Doubleday, 1971) and *What Is Contemplation?* (Springfield, Ill.: Templegate, 1978). More recently, Basil Pennington's books, *Daily We Touch Him, Centering Prayer,* and *A Place Apart,* have provided useful monastic insights into the practice of prayer for everyone.

In dealing with the question of how to integrate the life of prayer with the day-to-day experience of life outside the cloister, Evelyn Underhill, an Anglican writer and mystic of the early twentieth century, is a useful model and spiritual guide. To me, her most valuable book is *Practical Mysticism* (New York: E. P. Dutton & Co., first published 1915). Although contemporary readers will find it necessary to enter into a somewhat older vocabulary (rife with such terms as *mortification*), Underhill's great gift is her poetic spirit and plain insistence that even the practical person can be a contemplative in the midst of everything. "Look with the eye of contemplation," she advises, "on the most dissipated tabby of the streets, and you shall discern the celestial quality of life set like an aureole about his tattered ears. . . ."[2] Underhill's many books on mysticism are a fine contribution to the subject matter. However, these are not direct encouragements to the spiritual life. A less-known book, *The Spiritual Life* (New York, Harper & Row, n.d.) is as useful to the business of praying as *Practical Mysticism.*

Among mystical treatises, the one I cherish most is the anonymous fourteenth-century book *The Cloud of Unknowing.* William Johnston's translation (New York: Doubleday Image, 1973) is excellent, and the introduction provides valuable insights on parallels between this classic of Western mysticism and the experience of Eastern mystics. There are a number of books in this genre from earlier centuries now coming back into print. *A Mirror for Simple Souls,* by an anonymous thirteenth-century French mystic, was published in 1981 by Crossroad, New York, in a series that also includes such works as *A Letter of Private Direction* and *The*

Cell of Self-Knowledge, both early English mystical treatises. The value of such books, to me, is that they seem to be written from the point of view of one engaged in prayer. Even when the author is writing to instruct, the reader has a welcome sense that the eye of the instructor and that of the listener are both turned toward God.

William Johnston's books have been of real help to me. I mention in particular *The Still Point: Reflections on Zen and Christian Mysticism, Christian Zen, Silent Music,* and *The Inner Eye of Love.* Each of these books is a masterful blend of analytical writing about mystical experience, Eastern and Western, with an affirmation that prayer is real and within our reach.

Henri Nouwen's essay "Unceasing Prayer," published in *America* (August 5, 1978), is typical of the practical wisdom he has been able to convey about the practice of prayer. His book *Genesee Diary,* in which he recorded his experience as a "temporary monk," helped me to see prayer as a personal project, one that requires real commitment in space and time.

A very practical spirituality of radical dependence on God is contained in the program of Alcoholics Anonymous. The description of this God-centered program in *Twelve Steps and Twelve Traditions* (New York: Alcoholics Anonymous World Services, 1952) is carved out of life experience and can be of practical value to anyone who is struggling with other forms of dependency as well. Of special value is Step Eleven: "Sought through prayer and meditation to improve our conscious contact with God as we understood him, praying only for knowledge of his will for us and the power to carry that out." The twelfth step suggests that dependence upon God is essential in letting go of false dependencies, including overdependence on relatives and friends: "We found that dependence on his perfect justice, forgiveness, and love was healthy, and would work where nothing else would."

For its sheer practicality, the work of C. S. Lewis must also be mentioned, especially *Letters to Malcolm: Chiefly on Prayer* (New

York: Harcourt Brace Jovanovich, 1964). This extensive and helpful treatment of private prayer in the form of a correspondence with a friend anticipates many difficulties of ordinary persons who wish to build a sound and structured prayer-life. Lewis treats prayer often, touching on the subject in many of his works, and always insisting that prayer is within our reach and fundamental to the Christian life. Although he generally protests he is "not the one to speak," I have found him a fine spiritual mentor.

Richard Foster's books are fine spiritual guides. I would especially mention *Prayer: Finding the Heart's True Home* (San Francisco, CA: HarperSanFrancisco, 1992) and *A Celebration of Discipline* (San Francisco, CA: HarperSanFrancisco, 1988) The first provides an inventory of many ways of prayer. The second suggests a comprehensive approach to spiritual formation.

A contemporary spiritual guide who is extremely wise and practical is William Barry, who has written a number of short, pithy books about aspects of the spiritual life. I like especially *What Do I Want in Prayer?* (New York: Paulist Press, 1994) and *Finding God in All Things*.(Notre Dame, IN: Ave Maria Press, 1991.)

Finally, in designing a prayer-life, there is no more important book than the Bible. Jesus Christ is the model and master of our prayer. The disciples and apostles provide wise counsel. And one could do no better than to follow the path of the prophets and the writers of the Psalms.

NOTES

1. Andre Louf, *Teach Us to Pray: Learning a Little About God* (New York: Paulist Press, 1975), p. 19.
2. Evelyn Underhill, *Practical Mysticism* (New York: E.P. Dutton & Co., 1915), p. 94.

About the Author

Emilie Griffin is the author of a number of books on the spiritual life. She is a native of New Orleans and a veteran of the New York marketing world. It was there, when she and her husband were raising a young family and pursuing full-fledged careers, that she began seriously to pursue the life of prayer. She thinks it was partly personal crisis and partly providential. "I was first invited to prayer," she explains, "by others who were really praying, and were generous in sharing their prayer lives with me."

Emilie is the author of *Turning: Reflections on the Experience of Conversion; The Reflective Executive: a Spirituality of Business and Enterprise; Homeward Voyage: Reflections on Life-Changes; Wilderness Time: A Guide to Spiritual Retreat;* and *Doors into Prayer: an Invitation.* She has also edited *Spiritual Classics*, a collaboration with Richard Foster.

She is married to William Griffin, author of a major biography of C.S.Lewis and of new translations of *Thomas a Kempis, The Imitation of Christ* and *Augustine of Hippo: Sermons for the People.* The Griffins, who now live in Alexandria, Louisiana, are parents of three grown children and have two young grandchildren.